WORLD
HISTORY SERIES ▪▪▪

World War II
in the Pacific

Titles in the World History Series

WORLD
HISTORY SERIES

World War II
in the Pacific

by
Don Nardo

LUCENT BOOKS
SAN DIEGO, CALIFORNIA

THOMSON
━━━★━━━ ™
GALE

Detroit • New York • San Diego • San Francisco
Boston • New Haven, Conn. • Waterville, Maine
London • Munich

Cover photo: American casualties on Tarawa.

Library of Congress Cataloging-in-Publication Data

Nardo, Don, 1947–
    World War II in the Pacific / by Don Nardo.
        p.   cm.—(World history series)
Includes bibliographical references and index.
Summary: Discusses Japan's participation in World War II, in-
cluding militaristic advances and the bombing of Pearl
Harbor, its alliances, the use of the atomic bomb against it, and
its defeat and surrender.
        ISBN 1-59018-015-1 (hardback : alk. paper)
        1. World War, 1939–1945—Japan—Juvenile literature. 2.
Japan—History—1926–1945—Juvenile literature. 3. World
War, 1939–1945—Campaigns—Pacific Area—Juvenile litera-
ture 4. Atomic bomb—Juvenile literature. [1. World War.
1939–1945—Japan 2. Japan—History—1926–1945. 3. World
War, 1939–1945—Campaigns—Pacific Area.] I. Title: World
War II in the Pacific. II. Title: World War Two in the Pacific. III.
Title. IV. Series.
        D743.7 .N37 2002
        940.54'26—dc21

2001006606

Contents

Foreword

Each year on the first day of school, nearly every history teacher faces the task of explaining why his or her students should study history. One logical answer to this question is that exploring what happened in our past explains how the things we often take for granted—our customs, ideas, and institutions—came to be. As statesman and historian Winston Churchill put it, "Every nation or group of nations has its own tale to tell. Knowledge of the trials and struggles is necessary to all who would comprehend the problems, perils, challenges, and opportunities which confront us today." Thus, a study of history puts modern ideas and institutions in perspective. For example, though the founders of the United States were talented and creative thinkers, they clearly did not invent the concept of democracy. Instead, they adapted some democratic ideas that had originated in ancient Greece and with which the Romans, the British, and others had experimented. An exploration of these cultures, then, reveals their very real connection to us through institutions that continue to shape our daily lives.

Another reason often given for studying history is the idea that lessons exist in the past from which contemporary societies can benefit and learn. This idea, although controversial, has always been an intriguing one for historians. Those who agree that society can benefit from the past often quote philosopher George Santayana's famous statement, "Those who cannot remember the past are condemned to repeat it." Historians who subscribe to Santayana's philosophy believe that, for example, studying the events that led up to the major world wars or other significant historical events would allow society to chart a different and more favorable course in the future.

Just as difficult as convincing students of the importance of studying history is the search for useful and interesting supplementary materials that present historical events in a context that can be easily understood. The volumes in Lucent Books' World History Series attempt to present a broad, balanced, and penetrating view of the march of history. Ancient Egypt's important wars and rulers, for example, are presented against the rich and colorful backdrop of Egyptian religious, social, and cultural developments. The series engages the reader by enhancing historical events with these cultural contexts. For example, in *Ancient Greece*, the text covers the role of women in that society. Slavery is discussed in *The Roman Empire*, as well as how slaves earned their freedom. The numerous and varied aspects of everyday life in these and other societies are explored in each volume of the series. Additionally, the series covers the major political, cultural, and philosophical ideas as the torch of civilization is passed from ancient Mesopotamia and Egypt, through Greece, Rome, Medieval Europe, and other world cultures, to the modern day.

The material in the series is formatted in a thorough, precise, and organized manner. Each volume offers the reader a comprehensive and clearly written overview of an important historical event or period. The topic under discussion is placed in a broad, historical context. For example, *The Italian Renaissance* begins with a discussion of the High Middle Ages and the loss of central control that allowed certain Italian cities to develop artistically. The book ends by looking forward to the Reformation and interpreting the societal changes that grew out of the Renaissance. Thus, students are not only involved in an historical era, but also enveloped by the events leading up to that era and the events following it.

One important and unique feature in the World History Series is the primary and secondary source quotations that richly supplement each volume. These quotes are useful in a number of ways. First, they allow students access to sources they would not normally be exposed to because of the difficulty and obscurity of the original source. The quotations range from interesting anecdotes to farsighted cultural perspectives and are drawn from historical witnesses both past and present. Second, the quotes demonstrate how and where historians themselves derive their information on the past as they strive to reach a consensus on historical events. Lastly, all of the quotes are footnoted, familiarizing students with the citation process and allowing them to verify quotes and/or look up the original source if the quote piques their interest.

Finally, the books in the World History Series provide a detailed launching point for further research. Each book contains a bibliography specifically geared toward student research. A second, annotated bibliography introduces students to all the sources the author consulted when compiling the book. A chronology of important dates gives students an overview, at a glance, of the topic covered. Where applicable, a glossary of terms is included.

In short, the series is designed not only to acquaint readers with the basics of history, but also to make them aware that their lives are a part of an ongoing human saga. Perhaps then they will come to the same realization as famed historian Arnold Toynbee. In his monumental work, *A Study of History*, he wrote about becoming aware of history flowing through him in a mighty current, and of his own life "welling like a wave in the flow of this vast tide."

IMPORTANT DATES DURING
WORLD WAR II IN THE PACIFIC

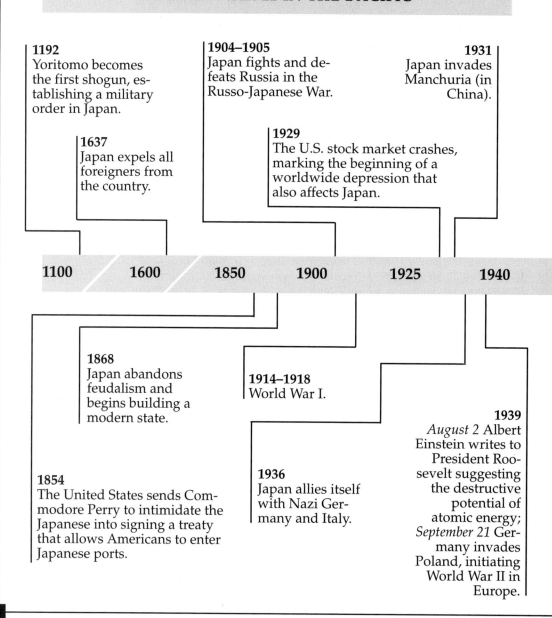

1192
Yoritomo becomes the first shogun, establishing a military order in Japan.

1637
Japan expels all foreigners from the country.

1904–1905
Japan fights and defeats Russia in the Russo-Japanese War.

1929
The U.S. stock market crashes, marking the beginning of a worldwide depression that also affects Japan.

1931
Japan invades Manchuria (in China).

1100   1600   1850   1900   1925   1940

1868
Japan abandons feudalism and begins building a modern state.

1914–1918
World War I.

1854
The United States sends Commodore Perry to intimidate the Japanese into signing a treaty that allows Americans to enter Japanese ports.

1936
Japan allies itself with Nazi Germany and Italy.

1939
August 2 Albert Einstein writes to President Roosevelt suggesting the destructive potential of atomic energy; *September 21* Germany invades Poland, initiating World War II in Europe.

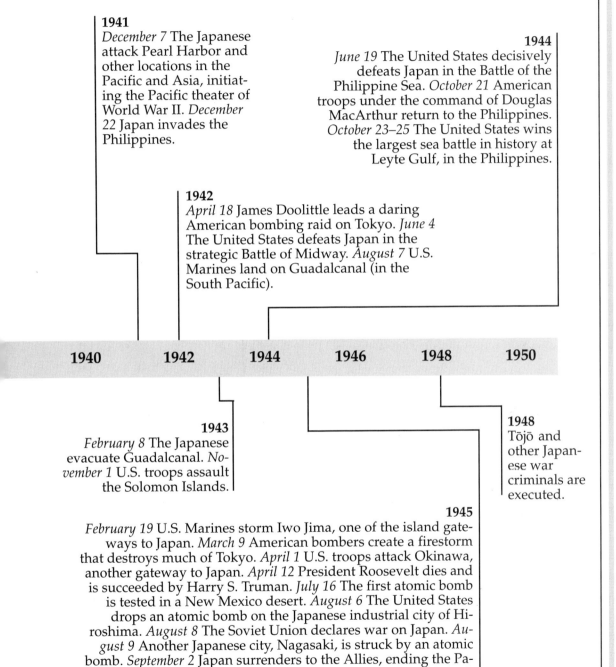

1941
December 7 The Japanese attack Pearl Harbor and other locations in the Pacific and Asia, initiating the Pacific theater of World War II. *December 22* Japan invades the Philippines.

1944
June 19 The United States decisively defeats Japan in the Battle of the Philippine Sea. *October 21* American troops under the command of Douglas MacArthur return to the Philippines. *October 23–25* The United States wins the largest sea battle in history at Leyte Gulf, in the Philippines.

1942
April 18 James Doolittle leads a daring American bombing raid on Tokyo. *June 4* The United States defeats Japan in the strategic Battle of Midway. *August 7* U.S. Marines land on Guadalcanal (in the South Pacific).

1940   1942   1944   1946   1948   1950

1943
February 8 The Japanese evacuate Guadalcanal. *November 1* U.S. troops assault the Solomon Islands.

1948
Tōjō and other Japanese war criminals are executed.

1945
February 19 U.S. Marines storm Iwo Jima, one of the island gateways to Japan. *March 9* American bombers create a firestorm that destroys much of Tokyo. *April 1* U.S. troops attack Okinawa, another gateway to Japan. *April 12* President Roosevelt dies and is succeeded by Harry S. Truman. *July 16* The first atomic bomb is tested in a New Mexico desert. *August 6* The United States drops an atomic bomb on the Japanese industrial city of Hiroshima. *August 8* The Soviet Union declares war on Japan. *August 9* Another Japanese city, Nagasaki, is struck by an atomic bomb. *September 2* Japan surrenders to the Allies, ending the Pacific War. *October 24* The United Nations is officially established.

Introduction

A Dangerous Clash of National Attitudes

At 1:40 P.M. on Sunday, December 7, 1941, Franklin D. Roosevelt, then serving his third term as president of the United States, was sitting and eating an apple in the White House study. Suddenly the phone rang. Leisurely picking it up, Roosevelt was surprised to hear that his secretary of the navy, Frank Knox, had an urgent message. The Department of the Navy, Knox said solemnly, had just received a dispatch from Hawaii reading,

"Air raid [at] Pearl Harbor. This is no drill."[1] The president learned that warplanes launched by the empire of Japan had suddenly and decisively attacked the U.S. naval base at Pearl Harbor in Hawaii. To Roosevelt's dismay, the casualties were reportedly heavy.

In the days that followed, hostilities in the Pacific Ocean sphere escalated as powerful and well-organized Japanese forces swept across several island chains and

Secretary of the Navy Frank Knox (right) called President Roosevelt on Sunday, December 7, 1941, to inform him of the Japanese attack on Pearl Harbor.

coastal regions of eastern Asia. The United States and its allies, who were already at war with Germany and Italy in the European sphere, responded by declaring war on Japan. And inside of a week, dozens of nations and nearly four-fifths of the people on earth were involved in the global conflict known as World War II.

Almost none of the nations involved had wanted the war with Japan, which became known as the Pacific War. Most Westerners—Americans, Canadians, British, and others—had done everything they could to avoid it. For the most part, they looked upon war as a destructive last resort for settling their differences with Japan and other nations. In contrast, the Japanese felt it was inevitable that they would become entangled in a war with the West. The view of war held by Japanese leaders was very different from that of Roosevelt, Great Britain's Winston Churchill, and other Western leaders. Japanese militarists, who had come to power in the 1930s, were fanatic in their belief that war was necessary, useful, and glorious. It was the only credible means of achieving Japan's "destiny" of ruling all of Asia and perhaps other continents. In their mind, it was better to die fighting enemies who stood in the way of that destiny than to live with the dishonor of never attaining it.

RESISTING THE WESTERN "BARBARIANS"

Such warlike attitudes stemmed partly from Japanese religious beliefs, which stressed that the gods favored the Japan-

British prime minister Winston Churchill and other western leaders had hoped to avoid war with Japan.

ese above all other peoples. In this view, foreigners were inferior "barbarians" who went against the natural order created by the gods. Therefore, it was only right and fitting that the Japanese should conquer or destroy those who threatened that order.

Japanese attitudes about war were also influenced by their culture. Since ancient times, the Japanese had glorified war itself. According to the *bushido*, the code developed by the samurai warrior class, to die in battle was the greatest possible honor; and to surrender in battle was the worst possible example of dishonor. Rather than accept either dishonor or surrender, a warrior was expected to commit suicide.

A particularly crucial factor was that the Japanese saw war with the West as a matter of self-defense. Japanese leaders viewed a major conflict as absolutely necessary to the survival of their country. They were convinced that the Western nations wanted to keep the Japanese weak and submissive while exploiting Japan's economic markets.

The ultimate goal of the United States, the Japanese believed, was to "Westernize" Japan and thereby destroy Japanese culture. According to this view, Japan must sooner or later confront, fight, and destroy the United States and other Western nations that threatened its existence.

Japanese leaders passed these ideas on to their people through a constant and effective campaign of propaganda. The government controlled what was reported in

Samurai warriors developed the bushido, *a code that influenced the Japanese attitudes about war.*

Japanese soldiers believed that waging war advanced their nation's honor.

the press and decided what would be taught in schools. Japanese children learned that Americans and other Westerners were arrogant, dishonorable, corrupt, and weak and could be defeated easily by the stronger, more ethical Japanese.

UNDERESTIMATING THE ENEMY

The Japanese were not the only ones who perpetrated such blatant distortions and stereotypes. On the other side of the Pacific, Americans had developed preconceived, usually inaccurate, and often racist notions about Japan and its people. As the late, noted historian Gordon Prange put it, most Americans saw the average Japanese as

> a funny little creature with buck teeth, strutting arrogantly over the map of Asia, a silly grin on his inscrutable [unreadable] face, with horn-rimmed glasses covering slanted slits of eyes. He bows so deeply his chin almost touches his knees. "So solly, please!". . . We [i.e., Americans] took insidious delight in poking fun at the Japanese and their country in cartoons, magazines, and newspapers.[2]

Perhaps more importantly, Americans and other Westerners did not see war as glorious or as an instrument to advance national honor, as the Japanese did. To the average American, war was disruptive and destructive and to be avoided if at all possible. In fact, until the Pacific War, U.S. soldiers had never faced an enemy so fanatic about war and so willing to die for honor. This was one of the reasons that the Americans were surprised by the attack on Pearl Harbor. Most of them believed as Pennsylvania congressman Charles Faddis did when only ten months before the attack he stated: "The Japanese are not going to risk a fight with a first-class nation [like the United States]. . . . They will not dare to get into a position where they must face the American navy in open battle."[3] This shows how unprepared Americans were for an adversary so willing to go to war, so ready to risk the fate of an entire nation in a bloody global conflict with larger nations.

Thus, the Pacific War was not only a huge and momentous military struggle, but also a dangerous clash of very different national attitudes about the nature and utility of war. For the United States, the conflict was a grim, unfortunate, but necessary fight against a sinister enemy. For Japan, by contrast, it was a glorious means of removing the chief obstacle on the road to an even more glorious destiny. Moreover, each side suffered more than was necessary because it began by grossly underestimating the strengths and abilities of the other. Had the United States taken the Japanese more seriously, it might have been more on its guard and avoided the tragedy at Pearl Harbor; conversely, if Japan had fully grasped the truly vast potential in military, logistical, and human resources possessed by the Americans, it might have thought twice about attacking them. Lacking the luxury of hindsight, however, the Japanese did attack; and to paraphrase one of their own leaders, they awoke a sleeping giant.

1 Sons of the Rising Sun: The Long Road to War

In the late 1930s, on the eve of World War II, the United States and Japan were two powerful nations uneasily facing each other across the wide Pacific Ocean. The United States, resting at the center of the North American continent, bordered the eastern side of the Pacific. U.S. influence extended to many countries in the Pacific area, largely because of ownership of the Hawaiian Islands, located about two thousand miles off the coast of California.

Bordering the western edge of the Pacific, at a distance of some five thousand miles from the United States, was the island nation of Japan. Located off the coast of Asia, Japan is a relatively small country. The combined total of its more than three thousand islands is an area slightly smaller than the state of California, barely one-twelfth the size of the United States.

The ocean was not the only barrier that separated the United States and Japan. Attitudes about politics and international relations were almost completely opposite in the two countries. The United States was one of the world's leading democracies, controlled by an elected president and congress. In the 1930s the country was largely isolationist, desiring to stay out of foreign disputes and wars.

By contrast, Japan was a dictatorship, ruled by a few powerful military leaders. The Japanese militarists were expansionists, seeking to extend their influence and control over other lands by any means necessary, including war. In fact, the Japanese leaders saw war with the United States and other "inferior" foreigners as essential to the continued survival and expansion of the Japanese people.

A Society of Warriors

Japan's traditions of militarism and hatred of foreigners, which ultimately plunged the world into war, had originated centuries before. For nearly two thousand years, the Japanese had recognized the absolute authority of a succession of emperors. Each one, the Japanese believed, was divine, descended directly from the sun-goddess Amaterasu. Eventually, the emperors came to wield little actual power; yet their prestige and moral authority with the people remained strong. Confident that the goddess favored their emperor and themselves above other peoples, the Japanese looked upon foreigners as inferior. To honor

THE EMPEROR'S DIVINITY

Historic evidence suggests that for as many as two thousand years, a succession of emperors has ruled Japan. For many centuries these rulers governed the land, made political policy, enforced laws, and waged war. In time, however, as powerful warlords transformed Japan into a feudal society, the role of the emperors became more ceremonial. Eventually, people regarded the emperor as a spiritual leader who stayed in the background and became involved in affairs of state only when absolutely necessary.

The shoguns and other Japanese leaders learned to take advantage of the spiritual image of the emperor. They pictured him as semidivine, having descended directly from the sun-goddess Amaterasu. Invoking the name of an emperor became an effective way to unify and control people. For instance, the shogun often convinced his emperor to endorse unpopular laws. People then tended to accept these laws as the will of the gods. Leaders also used the image of the emperor to instill feelings of pride and patriotism. The Japanese emperors were considered the only living gods in the world, and this made the Japanese people feel that they were special, favored by heaven above all other races.

This national worship of the emperor persisted into modern times. In 1890 the government declared in writing that the emperor was sacred and inviolable (untouchable). Elaborate rituals surrounded him. No one could look directly at the emperor when he passed by, and his personal name could never be spoken aloud. People swore complete allegiance to him, some even risking their lives to carry his picture out of burning buildings. To the pre–World War II Japanese, the emperor was a symbol of the country's honor and also a direct link between the people and the gods.

Amaterasu, Japanese leaders adopted the image of the sun as their special symbol and referred to their nation as the "land of the rising sun." They chose to remain isolated from foreign, "barbaric" nations and had little contact with the outside world.

Extreme militaristic attitudes took firm root in Japan beginning in the year 1185, when a powerful warlord named Minamoto Yoritomo seized control of most of the country. Seven years later the Japanese emperor, who was by this time merely a figurehead, bowed to Yoritomo's power and granted him the old military title of shogun (general). From this time on, with few exceptions, the shogun was the supreme authority in the country and his office, the shogunate, was by far the most prestigious.

Yoritomo established a formal military order in Japanese society, a new feudal order in which individual warlords ruled sections of the country and maintained forces of loyal warriors. The shogun oversaw these warlords. He was the absolute ruler of the country and, at least in theory, answered only to the emperor. In reality, because the emperor was thought to be a living god, he usually did not involve himself in everyday affairs unless the shogun requested him to do so. Meanwhile, the shogun allowed people to farm and fish in exchange for occasional military service.

For his permanent military staff, the shogun employed full-time professional warriors known as samurai. It was this samurai military order that planted the seeds of Japanese fanaticism about war. The samurai glorified war, believing that

Shogun Yoritomo (seated) established a formal military order in Japan when he seized control of the country in the late twelfth century.

DEATH WITH HONOR

Literally translated as "belly-cutting," hara-kiri was the common method of suicide practiced by the samurai and others in feudal Japan. Most Japanese prefer the older term *seppuku* to describe the ritual. The proper procedure was to stab a sword or knife into the left side of the stomach, slash across to the right side, then slice into the chest and push downward, forming a cross on the front of the body. If the person was still conscious after this, the last step was to cut the throat.

Because hara-kiri is a slow, painful form of suicide, it was thought to be a way of showing self-control and courage. Often samurai warriors committed hara-kiri after defeat in battle to avoid the dishonor of capture. Sometimes a warrior performed the ritual after the death of his lord in order to show loyalty. The tradition of hara-kiri survived along with the samurai code of honor into modern times. This was due to the popularity of plays like the eighteenth-century drama *Chushingura*, or the Tale of the Loyal Retainers. These plays glorify the idea of ritual suicide and influenced millions of ordinary Japanese citizens. Thousands of Japanese soldiers in World War II chose this form of death rather than surrender.

it was the most effective means of solving problems. They maintained a strict social code that emphasized loyalty and honor above all other virtues. A samurai owed complete allegiance to his shogun and to the emperor, for instance, and pledged to lay down his life for them if necessary. There was an intense pride about one's name and honor. When accused of dishonor, some samurai committed hara-kiri, or more accurately *seppuku*, a gruesome ritual suicide in which a knife or sword is plunged in and up through the stomach. Thus, noted scholar Edwin Reischauer explains, the proud samurai

formed a petty local aristocracy, somewhat like the knights of early feudal Europe, for they too were mounted, armored warriors. Their chief weapons were the bow and arrow, skillfully used from horseback, and the curved steel sword, which came to be the finest blade in the world. Their armor was quite different from that of the West, being much lighter and more flexible and therefore probably more efficient. It consisted largely of small strips of steel, bound together by brightly colored thongs and fitted loosely over the body.[4]

Most important from the standpoint of later generations, the samurai traditions of glorifying war and showing fanatic loyalty to the person in power steadily became a part of the character of the Japanese people as a whole.

THE OUTSIDE WORLD CLOSES IN

Japanese militaristic and antiforeign attitudes further intensified after the country started to deal with the outside world. Under the leadership of the shoguns, Japanese society had remained largely unchanged and isolated from other nations until the 1800s. This had profound effects on the development of Japanese culture. Unlike the Americans and many Europeans, the Japanese did not feel the influence of eighteenth-century social philosophers such as England's John Locke and France's Jean-Jacques Rousseau. Likewise, the Japanese knew little or nothing about in-

ventions such as the telescope, the steam engine, the cotton gin, and vaccines, which vastly changed ways of life in many other parts of the world. The birth of modern democracy in the wake of the American and French Revolutions of the late 1700s also escaped Japanese attention.

Even more significantly, the Japanese were ill prepared for contact with powerful British, French, American, and Russian commercial and military fleets that held virtual control of the world's seas by the early 1800s. In fact, scholar Neil Busch explains:

> Prisoners on their isolated islands for two hundred years . . . [the Japanese] rarely even caught sight of a foreign ship, and when they did it was only against a distant horizon. Since all ships look black when seen against the sky, this led future generations of Japanese to suppose that all foreign ships . . . were actually this color.

In 1853 Commodore Matthew Perry and several American warships arrived in Japan. Perry then demanded that the Japanese sign a treaty with the United States.

THE SAMURAI—PROUD WARRIORS

The samurai emerged as a distinct social class in Japan in the eleventh century. They were skillful, fearless warriors who trained for years to master the use of razor-sharp samurai swords and other forms of self-defense. Groups of samurai warriors were loyal to various powerful warlords and to the shoguns, who were themselves samurai. The samurai became the most feared, respected, and honored group in Japanese society.

Even after the rule of the shoguns ended in 1868, samurai influences remained. Among these were a strong sense of honor and a strict code of behavior that emphasized loyalty to authority, courage, and the choice of suicide over surrender. Most Japanese soldiers in World War II followed the samurai code of conduct enthusiastically.

"Black ships" became the generic term for them.[5]

By the early 1800s, the United States and other Western nations recognized that trade with Japan could be very lucrative. By opening a trade relationship, the United States could establish a valuable trade route to China. Also, U.S. whalers who hunted in the waters near Japan could use Japanese ports to resupply their ships. Moreover, Japan possessed many fine goods of its own, as well as numerous potential customers of foreign goods. Opening trade relations with Japan was seen, therefore, as an important first step in what could become a very profitable venture for Western nations.

The problem was that all attempts by British, Russian, and other Western agents to establish relations with Japanese leaders met with stern resistance. To overcome this resistance, the United States finally decided to resort to force. In 1853 Commodore Matthew Perry sailed a large squadron of American warships to Japan and demanded that the Japanese sign a treaty with the United States. The Japanese quickly indicated that they were not interested. But Perry made it clear in so many words that if the Japanese did not agree to the terms of the treaty, the United States would launch some kind of violent action. Intimidated by U.S. military might, Japanese leaders reluctantly signed the treaty in 1854, agreeing to allow American ships to resupply in Japanese ports. Seeing the opportunity to exploit Japanese markets, Britain and other nations immediately established trade relations with the Japanese, who now felt they had no choice but to cooperate.

THE INCREDIBLE TRANSFORMATION

As might be expected, the majority of Japanese were embarrassed and angry about the concessions made to the foreigners, believing that the outsiders would soon try to take over Japan. Japanese leaders decided that there was only one way their country could survive and prosper. It must become militarily and materially equal to Western countries like the United States.

In 1868, therefore, the Japanese began one of the most ambitious and enormous undertakings ever attempted by a nation. Their goal was to transform their backward country into a modern world power in the space of only a few years. As a first step, they abruptly abandoned feudalism and emphasized nationalism—loyalty to the nation instead of loyalty to individual warlords and shoguns. Loyalty to the emperor was also stressed, for the Japanese still looked upon him as a living god. The militarists called on all Japanese to unite behind the emperor, who would for the first time in many centuries, they claimed, assume a measure of real authority. The fifteen-year-old emperor, Mutsuhito, took the reign title of Meiji, meaning "enlightened rule," so the supposed return to imperial rule became known as the Meiji Restoration. This was only a ploy, of course, for the

military leaders fully intended to make all the important decisions themselves and keep the emperor as a figurehead. Since the term "oligarchy" refers to rule by an elite group of individuals, historians often call the powerful lords who now controlled both the emperor and the Japanese state the Meiji oligarchs.

Thus, although the feudal rule of the shoguns had been eliminated, Japan was still very much under the thumb of a powerful military elite. If nothing else, its members were certainly highly organized and efficient. In only two decades, they managed completely to restructure the country's political, military, and educational institutions, forcing all Japanese to work toward a single national aim. That aim was to make the country as strong as possible. For example, schoolchildren were taught that the Japanese must be strong and aggressive in order to survive in a world swarming with hostile foreigners. In addition, the government built many factories that began to manufacture modern ships, guns, and other weapons. To help pay for these advances, the Japanese borrowed heavily from U.S. and other foreign banks. Eventually, Japan repaid many of these debts and maintained sizable investments in these banks.

Japan wanted to use its new weapons to expand its borders, which amounted to a complete reversal of its former isolationism. Believing that the country needed fresh land and resources to make it more powerful, the new government became aggressive and tried to expand into neighboring countries. For hundreds of years,

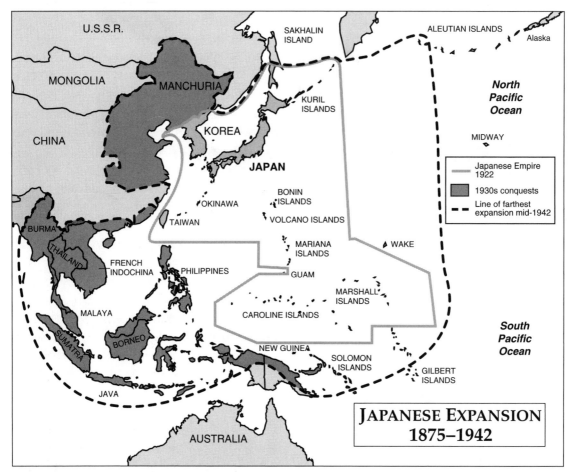

JAPANESE EXPANSION 1875–1942

Legend:
- Japanese Empire 1922
- 1930s conquests
- Line of farthest expansion mid-1942

Japan had been an empire only in name. Now, under the grasping and relentless Meiji oligarchs, it would become an empire in fact.

The powerful, modernized Japanese army fought wars against China (1894–95) and Russia (1904–05) and won both conflicts. From the Chinese, Japan gained the island of Formosa (now Taiwan), south of Japan. From the Russians, the Japanese gained control of Korea, located only a few miles west of the Japanese home islands. After defeating Russia, the Japanese bragged openly that they had destroyed the myth of the supposed superiority of the white race.

CONTINUED JAPANESE AGGRESSION

After Japan's victories over China and Russia, the surprised Western countries recognized that Japan was a real and quite threatening military power in the Far East. Thereafter, whenever possible, the Western countries tried to limit that power. In 1922, for example, shortly after the end of World War I, an international conference was held in Washington, D.C., to establish limits on weapons. One of the resolutions voted on by the Western powers in this so-called Washington Conference placed a limit on the number of warships Japan could build. According to the agreement that the major powers more or less forced on Japan, for every five warships built by the United States, Britain could also build five, but Japan could build only three.

Needless to say, this greatly angered the Japanese, who believed that the United States and its allies wanted to keep Japan weak and submissive. Japan's extreme militarists used this incident and others to fuel warlike attitudes among the Japanese people. They sought to carry on the ancient samurai warrior traditions and strike back at any and all who opposed them. One Japanese official threatened, "Japan must no longer let the impudence of the white man go unpunished."[6]

Making good on this threat, the Japanese began a new series of warlike maneuvers. The first was the sudden and brutal invasion of the Chinese province of Manchuria in 1931. The Japanese felt that the invasion was justified, partly because it would help ensure the continued survival and prosperity of Japan. Between 1868 and 1930, Japan's population had risen from 30 million to more than 65 million, and the country badly needed coal, oil, farmland, and other resources that Manchuria possessed in abundance. The Japanese militarists also justified the invasion on the grounds that the Japanese had a right to exploit "inferior" peoples. One member of the government claimed, "From the fact of divine descent of the Japanese people proceeds their immeasurable superiority to the natives of other countries in courage and intelligence."[7]

In addition, the incident, as well as later Japanese aggressions, was characterized by a decidedly racial dimension. Japan's leaders claimed that their acts and policies were ultimately for the good of all Asians, who, without Japanese "help," would eventually be overrun by the Western "barbarians." Using slogans such as "Asia for the Asians," the militarists sought to exclude Western influences not only from Japan, but also from Asia itself.

There was little opposition to Japan's aggression in China. The Chinese were too weak militarily to fight back in any meaningful way and appealed to the Western powers for help. But because they were preoccupied with the problems of the Great Depression, which had begun in 1929, the United States, Britain, and other countries hardly reacted to the takeover of Manchuria. They verbally condemned the action, but they allowed Japan to keep its prize. This emboldened Japanese leaders; and in 1932 they made Manchuria into a Japanese-governed state, changing its name to Manchukuo. They also continued to build up their armed forces, producing thousands of warplanes and hundreds of modern ships, in direct violation of the 1922 shipbuilding ban.

In 1936 and 1937, Japan made three more hostile moves. In each instance, the United States and other Western powers failed to act decisively against the growing Japanese threat. First, the Japanese signed an agreement of mutual cooperation, called the Anti-Comintern Pact, with the German Nazis led by Adolf

Hitler. Second, Japan invaded the heartland of China, intending to gain control of more valuable natural resources and farmland. Third, Japan joined Germany and Italy, two other militaristic states, to form the Axis powers. Each vowed to support the others if they were attacked. Because the three countries showed hostile intentions and were heavily arming themselves, most other nations saw the Axis alliance as a disturbing threat to world peace.

Japanese troops enter Manchuria. This invasion was the first in a series of maneuvers designed to ensure the continued survival and prosperity of Japan.

FRANKLIN D. ROOSEVELT

The thirty-second president of the United States, Franklin Delano Roosevelt (1882–1945) served three full terms and part of a fourth, longer than any other president. He was one of the most important and influential leaders of the twentieth century. Roosevelt came from a wealthy family and worked his way up through various political offices, including state senator, assistant secretary of the navy, and governor of New York.

Although stricken with polio and confined to a wheelchair, Roosevelt courageously ran for president in 1932. He promised to get the country out of the devastating depression that had begun with the crash of the stock market in 1929. He won a decisive victory and immediately implemented his New Deal, a national program of economic reform and recovery. By the late 1930s, the country's financial situation had improved, and Roosevelt became increasingly popular with the American people.

During World War II Roosevelt was a strong leader who effectively helped forge and maintain the Allied partnership against the Axis powers. He became known as a defender of democracy in the United States and around the world. And he bolstered people's courage during the most difficult days of the war by saying that the only thing they had to  fear was fear itself. Freedom-loving people around the world were stunned and saddened when Roosevelt died of a stroke in April 1945, shortly before the Allied victory he had worked so tirelessly to achieve.

President Franklin Delano Roosevelt was a strong and effective leader.

AMERICAN ATTITUDES BEGIN TO CHANGE

The main reason that the United States did not act to stop Japan's numerous acts of aggression was that the Americans wanted to stay out of foreign disputes whenever possible. The United States had not always had this attitude. In the 1800s the country had often sought to expand its influence and holdings in other parts of the world. But by the early 1900s, many Americans had expressed less and less enthusiasm for the country getting involved in affairs in little-known, far-away lands.

As a result, when World War I erupted in Europe in 1914 U.S. leaders were reluctant to commit the nation to fighting. Although the United States eventually did fight in the war, most Americans felt that too many fellow citizens had died battling for foreign causes. The United States became so disillusioned by World War I that in 1928 American officials signed the Kellogg-Briand Pact, an international document condemning war as a means of national policy. As a result, during the period in which Japan moved from isolationism to expansionism, the United States followed nearly the opposite course.

By the late 1930s, Americans perceived that another war was brewing in Europe. And most of them clearly did not want to become involved. Reflecting this growing national attitude, between 1935 and 1937 Congress passed a series of neutrality laws aimed at keeping the country out of foreign wars.

HIDEKI TŌJŌ

For Americans during World War II, Hideki Tōjō (1884–1948) became a symbol of Japanese fanaticism and militarism. The phrase "defeating Tōjō " became synonymous with defeating Japan itself. Nicknamed the Razor by his supporters, Tōjō was the son of a samurai. He was therefore loyal to the ancient Japanese code of honor and believed that the Japanese were superior to other peoples. In the late 1930s, Tōjō led a group of Japanese militarists who wanted to see Japan aggressively expand into Asia and the Pacific. He became war minister in 1940 and in October 1941 premier of Japan. He had nearly total control of the Japanese war effort until his resignation in 1944. Captured by the Americans after the war, Tōjō tried to commit hara-kiri but failed and was later executed for his role in waging the war.

THE FATAL MARCH TOWARD WAR

In 1939, as many people in the United States had feared, war broke out in Europe. Adolf Hitler's deadly Nazi forces invaded Poland, shattering the peace of the world. With their German allies displaying such bold initiative, Japanese military leaders became more confident than ever about Japan's aggressive policies. In 1940 Hideki Tōjō, a fanatic militarist, became Japan's war minister. Tōjō strongly believed that the Japanese should live by the samurai code of honor. Loudly citing the "Asia for the Asians" doctrine that Japan had recently developed, he warned that non-Asian people like the Americans and British had no right to interfere with affairs in eastern Asia, including strategic Indochina (now Vietnam).

Shortly after taking power, Tōjō and his henchmen followed up on this warning by announcing the formation of the Greater East Asia Co-Prosperity Sphere. In their words, Japan would liberate the members of the sphere—the residents of Indochina and other Asian lands—from "Western bondage." In reality, of course, these lands were earmarked as Japanese colonies to be taken by conquest. "Reduced to its essentials," historian Edwin P. Hoyt remarks, this plan "meant rice for Japan. There would be a little tin, a little rubber, a little sugar. But Indochina was the major rice-exporting area of Southeast Asia, and as such [it was] invaluable to a hungry Japan."[8]

Tōjō and his supporters were convinced that the United States, with so many economic interests in the area, was the main stumbling block in their plans to take over most of the countries of eastern Asia and the Pacific region. Sooner or later, they believed, they would have to confront the Americans. Japanese leaders made sure their people did not forget about how the United States had humiliated Japan in the 1800s and continually referred to America as Japan's mortal enemy.

The confrontation between the two countries came much sooner than even Tōjō expected. In July 1941 the Japanese marched troops into Indochina to seize the area's vast stretches of rice paddies. The American president, Franklin D. Roosevelt, sternly warned the Japanese to get out. And when they refused, he ordered that all Japanese money invested in American banks be frozen, that is, locked up and rendered inaccessible. This meant that the Japanese could not use their own money to buy important supplies and armaments. Other countries followed Roosevelt's lead and froze Japanese investments. Enraged, Tōjō and other Japanese leaders decided that there was only one way that Japan could continue to survive and prosper. It must eliminate the United States as an economic and military threat; in the name of honor, Japan must attack.

A SECRET ARMADA

In the following months, the United States continued to express its public opposition to Japanese aggression. But the Americans still hoped to avoid war and attempted to create a diplomatic solution. U.S. leaders had no way of knowing that the Japanese had already made up their minds to fight. Even while peace talks between the two countries were going on, the Japanese secretly assembled a huge fleet of seventy-two warships, carrying hundreds of planes and thousands of tons of bombs.

On November 26, 1941, this mighty armada sailed under the command of Admiral Chuichi Nagumo from Japan's Kuril Islands. Maintaining radio silence so as not to warn American planes and ships, the force headed for Hawaii's Pearl Harbor, where almost the entire U.S. Pacific Fleet lay anchored. The plan seemed simple. The sons of the rising sun would destroy American military power in the Pacific in one bold stroke. Then, the Japanese gods willing, nothing could stand in the way of Japan's glorious dreams of conquest.

Chapter

2 "Climb Mount Niitaka": The Attack on Pearl Harbor

On Sunday morning, December 7, 1941, all but three of the huge warships of the U.S. Pacific Fleet lay anchored in Pearl Harbor on the Hawaiian island of Oahu. The USS *Arizona, West Virginia, Oklahoma, California, Maryland,* and many other heavily armored vessels, along with smaller cruisers and destroyers, lined the docks of the harbor. Altogether, ninety-six ships were anchored at the Pearl Harbor naval base. Missing that fateful morning were the *Colorado,* in dry dock on the U.S. West Coast, and the aircraft carriers *Lexington* and *Enterprise,* which were at sea. Meanwhile, rows of military barracks, administrative and maintenance buildings, as well as civilian houses stretched along the coast to the harbor. And nearly four hundred American bombers and fighter planes were parked, wingtip to wingtip, on nearby airfields. To the shock and dismay of American officials and the world in general, by the end of that fateful morning nearly all of this vital array of weaponry—the United States' bastion of defense in the Pacific—would be destroyed.

THE AMERICANS: UNPREPARED AND UNINFORMED

The enormous scope of the disaster was made worse by the fact that almost no one expected it. By 7:00 A.M. on the seventh, some American personnel at the Pearl Harbor base were already eating breakfast or getting ready for church. But most were still asleep or lounging in their bunks. The general mood was calm because no one on the base had any reason to suspect trouble from any nation, including Japan. Everyone knew that American-Japanese relations had been strained since the Japanese invasion of Indochina the previous July. But Japan was thousands of miles away, and the Americans at Pearl Harbor assumed there would be weeks of advance notice if Hawaii was to be threatened.

In retrospect, it is now clear that there *were* a few tantalizing warning signs of the impending assault; but the American personnel assigned to spy on the Japanese and interpret their decoded messages either did not understand their significance or failed to inform the proper authorities

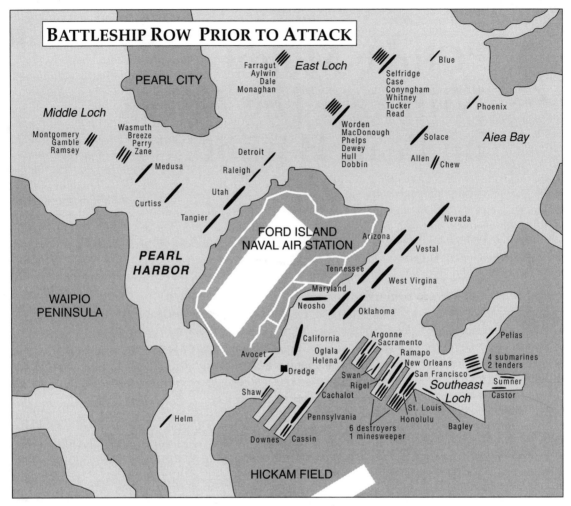

BATTLESHIP ROW PRIOR TO ATTACK

PEARL CITY

Middle Loch

East Loch

Blue

Farragut
Aylwin
Dale
Monaghan

Selfridge
Case
Conyngham
Whitney
Tucker
Read

Phoenix

Montgomery
Gamble
Ramsey

Wasmuth
Breeze
Perry
Zane

Worden
MacDonough
Phelps
Dewey
Hull
Dobbin

Solace

Aiea Bay

Detroit

Medusa

Raleigh

Allen Chew

Curtiss

Utah

Nevada

Tangier

FORD ISLAND
NAVAL AIR STATION

Arizona

Vestal

PEARL
HARBOR

Tennessee

West Virginia

WAIPIO
PENINSULA

Maryland

Neosho

Oklahoma

California

Argonne
Sacramento

Pelias

Avocet

Oglala
Helena

Ramapo
New Orleans

4 submarines
2 tenders

Dredge

Swan
Rigel

San Francisco

Southeast
Loch

Sumner

Shaw

Cachalot

St. Louis

Castor

Helm

Pennsylvania

Honolulu

Bagley

Downes Cassin

6 destroyers
1 minesweeper

HICKAM FIELD

in time. In September 1941 the Department of the Navy intercepted a message sent from Tokyo to the Japanese consulate in Honolulu, Hawaii. It ordered the chief Japanese official there to report regularly on the number, kinds, and movements of U.S. ships at Pearl Harbor. The chief of the Far Eastern sector of U.S. Army intelligence, Colonel Rufus Bratton, received a copy of the message and considered it important. "The Japanese were showing unusual interest in the port of Honolulu," he said later.[9] However, Bratton's immediate superiors felt there was nothing to the message and failed to pass it along to Husband E. Kimmel, commander of the U.S. fleet. Moreover, even if Kimmel *had* seen the message, in all likelihood he would not have assumed that an attack on Hawaii was imminent. After all, there had been no concrete indications that the Japanese were mounting a major naval operation.

A good deal more suspicious was a Japanese message intercepted early in the morning of December 7, the day of the

THE JAPANESE ATTACK PLANES

During the 1920s and 1930s, the Japanese built one of the most modern and effective air forces in the world. U.S. aviation experts knew that the Japanese were building large numbers of planes. But the Americans greatly underestimated the worth of Japanese attack planes, assuming that the Japanese planes were poor copies of American versions. Said a U.S. military expert in 1938, "The [Japanese] ability to produce original [aircraft] designs is lacking." When the war began, the Americans were stunned by the superiority of Japanese warplanes.

Of the many types of fighter aircraft the Japanese designed, the world-famous Zero was the most formidable. The Zero, which first saw service in 1940, was the first carrier-based fighter plane that could perform as well as land-based planes. It could fly at 330 mph, making it the fastest attack plane in the world when it was built. With its speed, superior firepower, and an ability to climb quickly and maneuver easily, the Zero was much more effective than any of the American planes during the early days of the war. Its one weakness was that it was constructed of lightweight materials and had no armor. This meant that even a minor hit could destroy it. Although American planes eventually surpassed it in speed and firepower, for at least two years, the Zero was the terror of the Pacific skies.

Other effective Japanese attack planes were the AICHI Type 99 carrier bomber, nicknamed the "Val" by the Allies, and the B5N2 Type 97 carrier bomber, nicknamed the "Kate." The Val flew at 240 mph, much slower than the Zero, but maneuvered unusually well. Vals sank more Allied warships than any other Axis planes during World War II. The Kates were deadly torpedo planes, each of which could carry a 1,764-pound torpedo. When one of these powerful torpedoes struck an Allied ship in the right place, the vessel was doomed.

Japan's fighter plane, the Zero, was more effective than any American planes early in the war.

attack. It instructed Japan's ambassador in Washington, D.C., to inform the U.S. government at precisely 1:00 P.M. eastern time that the Japanese were breaking off relations with the United States; furthermore, the ambassador was to destroy his code machine. "Again," writes historian Ronald H. Spector,

> it was Colonel Bratton who grasped the significance of the message. He was struck by the fact that it was to be delivered on a Sunday and that Tokyo had, for the first time, specified a precise hour. The colonel was convinced that the delivery time was intended to coincide with a Japanese attack on some American installation in the Far East, probably the Philippines. . . . Bratton frantically attempted to reach [army] Chief of Staff [George C.] Marshall and his assistants but was unable to reach the general for almost an hour because Marshall had gone for his Sunday morning horseback ride.[10]

Two and a half hours later, Bratton finally showed Marshall the messages and the chief of staff ordered that a warning be transmitted to U.S. bases in the Far East. Because of some technical foul-ups, however, the warning was not marked "Priority" and did not reach Hawaii until shortly after the attack was over.

JAPANESE CONCERNS

These American misjudgments and mistakes played right into the hands of Japa-

nese war planners and ensured that the attack would be a devastating surprise. At precisely 7:02 A.M. Hawaii time on the morning of December 7, an Army Air Corps radar operator detected a large group of planes approaching Oahu from the north at a distance of about 137 miles. The operator quickly telephoned his duty officer, Lieutenant Kermit Tyler. Tyler knew that a flight of American B-17 bombers had left California on December 6 and were due to arrive that morning on Oahu. Thinking that these were the planes that had been sighted, he told the radar man, "Don't worry about it."[11]

What Tyler and his coworkers had no way of knowing was that the approaching planes were actually Japanese. The fighters were on their last leg of a top-secret journey that Japan's senior naval officers had planned in September. The pilots had been briefed on October 5 and had sailed, along with their planes, on the warships of Admiral Chuichi Nagumo's mighty fleet. (Best estimates by historians suggest the task force contained 6 aircraft carriers, 2 battleships, 2 heavy cruisers, 1 light cruiser, 9 destroyers, 3 submarines, 8 tankers, and 432 planes, 353 of which would take part in the raid. In addition, an advance force of 28 submarines had already been dispatched; their mission was to destroy any American ships that attempted to enter or leave Pearl Harbor during and immediately after the attack.) On December 5, at a secret rendezvous point in the Pacific Ocean north of Hawaii, the fleet received the coded radio message "Climb Mount Niitaka." This was the or-

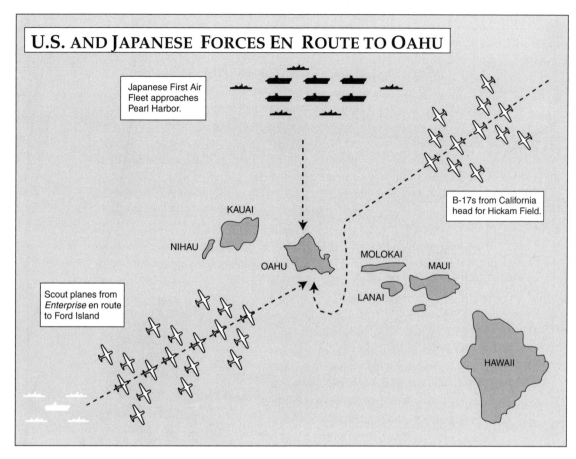

U.S. AND JAPANESE FORCES EN ROUTE TO OAHU

Japanese First Air Fleet approaches Pearl Harbor.

B-17s from California head for Hickam Field.

KAUAI

NIHAU

OAHU

MOLOKAI

MAUI

LANAI

Scout planes from *Enterprise* en route to Ford Island

HAWAII

der to proceed with the surprise attack on the American base.

The Japanese operation had obviously been extremely well thought-out and well organized, else so large a task force would not have been able to proceed so far under the cloak of nearly complete secrecy. Nevertheless, even after the mission was well under way, various Japanese officers involved expressed misgivings or worries about the plan's efficiency and likelihood of success. For example, Isoroku Yamamoto, supreme commander of Japan's fleets, did not like the idea of sending so many submarines in advance of the main fleet. He worried that they might be too easily detected and tip off

the Americans to the assault. But his superiors in Tokyo, who wrongly believed that the subs would do more damage than airpower, overruled him.

Another Japanese officer, Gunichi Mikawa, commander of the battleships and cruisers in the task force, was worried that he did not have enough battleships. "Frankly, I was apprehensive," he later recalled.

With just two battleships . . . under my command, I was operating with no margin of security at all. Our carriers were for the most part still untested, but I knew what fourteen- and sixteen-inch

Minoru Genda, Master of Air Attack

When the Japanese admirals began to plot the attack on Pearl Harbor, they put Minoru Genda in charge of the planning. A thirty-six-year-old aviation expert, Genda had formerly served in the Japanese embassy in London. There, he carefully studied Great Britain's successful use of airpower. Genda told the admirals that the Pearl Harbor plan, code-named Operation Z, was risky but still possible. He worked out the details with Mitsuo Fuchida, who actually led the attack. Later Fuchida commented, "Genda wrote the script. My pilots and I produced it." Genda was able to coordinate a major air strike while maintaining complete radio silence. He remembered seeing a newsreel that showed four U.S. carriers moving together in close formation. The Americans signaled to each other using flags and spotlights. The Japanese, concluded Genda, could use these same tactics while launching planes against Pearl Harbor. In 1942 Genda planned the Japanese strategy for the Battle of Midway. He served his country again after the war as the head of the air force defense system from 1959 to 1962.

Minoru Genda was the chief planner of the Japanese attack on Pearl Harbor.

shells could do. I feared interception at sea [by American warships] and possible surface action . . . and I was convinced that my . . . ships would be inadequate to protect our carriers in case the U.S. fleet closed in.[12]

Fortunately for Mikawa, the scenario he feared never transpired.

Even some of the Japanese pilots felt the plan had flaws. On the morning of November 23, Nagumo ordered all officers, commanders, and pilots in the fleet to assemble on his vessel, the *Akagi*, for a discussion of the details of the attack. One speaker, Lieutenant Commander Kenjiro Ono, explained that the pilots needed to maintain radio silence whenever possible;

but if they experienced engine failure or some other serious problem, they could briefly radio their positions to the fleet. At this point, the leader of the Eleventh Dive-Bombing Group leaped to his feet and cried, "I object to this plan of breaking radio silence no matter what the reasons might be at the moment of such a decisive battle which is to do or die for Japan!" Turning to his pilots, he said, "What about this? Why don't we die in silence if our engines conk out?"[13] The commander went on to suggest that the fleet should not respond to any appeals for help, even after the end of the attack; and a few minutes later, the pilots agreed to a man that they would gladly die for their country rather than risk giving away the fleet's position to the enemy. Such was the power of the warrior ethic that had been instilled in countless generations of Japanese men.

THE FIRST WAVE OF DESTRUCTION

All such concerns having been laid to rest, early in the morning of December 7, the Japanese planes lifted off their carriers and headed for Pearl Harbor. Mitsuo Fuchida, commander and leader of the attackers, flew ahead of the other planes to scout the target. He arrived high over Oahu at 7:53 A.M. and saw the American ships lined up like sitting ducks below. Excitedly, he radioed back to the other planes, "Tora! Tora! Tora!" [Tiger! Tiger! Tiger!], which signified the successful achievement of complete surprise.

At about 8:00 A.M., a huge squadron of 189 Japanese planes swarmed like angry hornets over Oahu's volcano, Diamond Head, and swooped down on the unsuspecting Americans. Torpedo planes and dive-bombers began raining explosives on the warships in the harbor, while fighter planes attacked the airfields. American first reactions were typified by that of Seaman First Class Short, who was writing Christmas cards at his machine-gun station aboard the USS *Maryland:*

> Suddenly I noticed planes diving on the Naval Air Base nearby. At first I thought they were our planes just in mock diving practice attack, but when I saw smoke and flames rising from a building, I looked closer and saw that they were not American planes. I broke out the ammunition nearby, loaded my machine gun and opened fire on two torpedo planes coming in from the east.[14]

At Pearl Harbor and other locations on Oahu, startled American sailors, marines, and assorted military personnel scrambled to mount a defense; but they were hindered by deafening noise, smoke, flames, and mass confusion. The Japanese attackers roamed at will, blowing up barracks, hangars, and houses, as well as ships and planes. They spread a wave of destruction as they went.

Admiral Kimmel, whose subordinates had earlier failed to show him the intercepted Japanese message, was in his home on a hill overlooking the harbor. Suddenly, his duty officer, Commander Vincent Murphy, rushed in and told him, "There's a

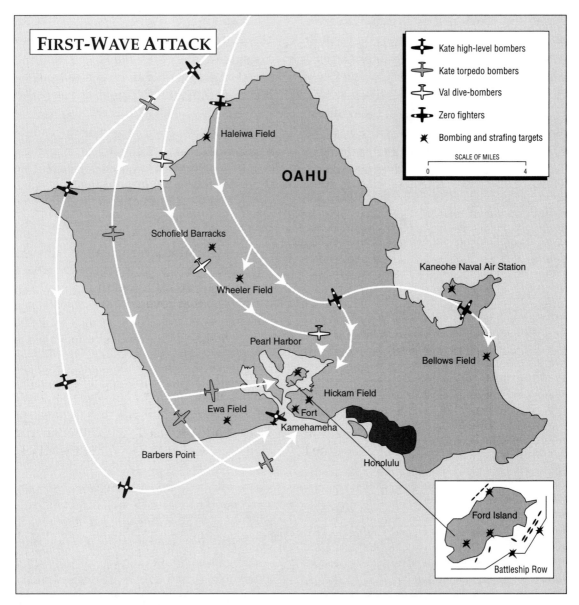

FIRST-WAVE ATTACK

Kate high-level bombers
Kate torpedo bombers
Val dive-bombers
Zero fighters
Bombing and strafing targets

SCALE OF MILES
0   4

OAHU

Haleiwa Field

Schofield Barracks

Wheeler Field

Kaneohe Naval Air Station

Pearl Harbor

Bellows Field

Ewa Field

Hickam Field

Fort
Kamehameha

Barbers Point

Honolulu

Ford Island

Battleship Row

message from the signal tower saying the Japanese are attacking Pearl Harbor, and this is no drill!"[15] Fumbling to button his shirt, Kimmel ran into his garden and watched helplessly as, one by one, the American warships were struck by bombs.

The USS *Arizona* suffered some of the worst damage of all, taking a hit in its for-

ward section. One eyewitness saw the ship "lift out of the water, then sink back down—way down."[16] Then, as historian Walter Lord tells it:

A huge ball of fire and smoke mush-roomed 500 feet into the air. . . . Hundreds of men were cut down in a single, searing flash. Inside the port antiaircraft director, one fire control man simply vanished. . . . On the bridge, Rear Admiral Isaac C. Kidd and Captain Franklin Van Valkenburgh were instantly killed. On the second deck, the entire ship's band was wiped out. Over 1000 men were gone.[17]

Like sharks sensing spilled blood, more Japanese fighters closed in and rained a barrage of bombs on the doomed *Arizona*. Fewer than three hundred of its crew of some fifteen hundred made it out alive.

Massive explosions repeatedly rocked the other ships. U.S. commander Jesse Kenworth, serving aboard the *West Virginia*, recalled:

As I reached the upper deck, I felt a very heavy shock and heard a loud explosion and the ship immediately began to list to port. Oil and water descended on the deck and by the time I

had reached the boat deck, the shock of two more explosions on the port side was felt. As I attempted to get to the Conning Tower over decks slippery with oil . . . I felt the shock of another heavy explosion.[18]

Meanwhile, the *Oklahoma* was hit by three torpedoes and quickly capsized, turning bottom-up and taking four hundred men to their deaths. The *California, Maryland, Tennessee,* and many other ships sustained heavy damage and numerous casualties. Many sailors jumped from their sinking ships in desperation, only to be burned to death in a mass of blazing oil that covered the surface of the harbor.

Meanwhile, the relentless attackers destroyed nearly all the planes on the airfields, making it impossible for the Americans to muster a credible counterattack. The flight of B-17s that Lieutenant Tyler had confused with the enemy planes arrived at the height of the attack,

The USS Arizona *(right) sinks after coming under heavy Japanese fire.*

but they carried no ammunition and could do nothing to help. Shot at by Japanese fighter planes, the B-17s barely managed to land safely on the badly damaged airfields.

THE DEADLY SECOND WAVE

By 8:30 A.M. the attackers had spent their ammunition and departed. Fearing that another attack was coming, the American defenders desperately raced to set up antiaircraft guns and other defenses. Their fears were confirmed when, shortly before 9:00 A.M., a second wave of Japanese planes, consisting of 175 bombers and fighters, appeared and mercilessly resumed the assault. The *Pennsylvania, Cassin, Downes, Shaw,* and several other American ships now suffered serious damage. In addition, some of the attackers flew low and fired at people running along the ground.

When the Japanese finally withdrew at about 10:00 A.M., Mitsuo Fuchida continued to circle overhead, photographing the results of the raid. "A warm feeling came," he later said,

> with the realization that the reward [of all the planning and training] . . . was unfolded before my eyes. I counted four battleships definitely sunk and

THE SINKING OF THE *ARIZONA*

On the morning of December 7, 1941, the great battleship USS *Arizona* floated beside its sister ships of the Pacific Fleet in Pearl Harbor, Hawaii. Ensign G.S. Flannigan remembered how an air raid siren suddenly broke the morning calm. "I was in the bunk room," recalled Flannigan, "and everyone thought it was a joke to have an air raid on Sunday. Then I heard an explosion." Within minutes dozens of Japanese planes homed in on the *Arizona* and released a deadly rain of bombs and torpedoes. One bomb fell directly into one of the vessel's funnels. Seconds later the ship's "forward magazines blew up with a tremendous explosion and large sheets of flame shot skyward," according to one eyewitness. Burning debris from this blast landed on the nearby USS *Tennessee,* and ignited raging fires. More than twelve hundred of the *Arizona*'s crew, including Admiral Isaac C. Kidd, died in the attack. The ship went down, forever entombing many of the victims at the bottom of the harbor. After the war a monument was erected atop the *Arizona*'s sunken bridge in honor of those who lost their lives.

The destroyer USS Shaw explodes after being hit by Japanese bombs. Eighteen ships were sunk or badly damaged in the attack.

three severely damaged, and extensive damage had also been inflicted upon other types of ships. The seaplane base at Ford Island was all in flames, as were the airfields, especially Wheeler Field.[19]

The much-satisfied Fuchida took pictures for nearly an hour, then turned his plane northward toward the waiting Japanese fleet.

Fuchida and his pilots left behind a scene of utter devastation. The base at Pearl Harbor lay in ruins. Giant columns of black smoke billowed from the twisted hulks of the crippled ships, and the bodies of the dead and dying sailors floated in the water and littered the docks. Fuchida's initial estimate had been conservative. Eighteen ships had been sunk or badly damaged and 308 planes destroyed or put out of action. The human toll: 2,343 Americans dead, 1,272 wounded, and almost 1,000 miss-

ing. Half of the entire U.S. Navy had been wiped out, and American military power in the Pacific was effectively paralyzed. In stunning contrast, the Japanese had lost a mere 29 planes. The victory was clearly overwhelming and decisive.

SHOCK AND OUTRAGE

When the news of the Pearl Harbor attack reached Japan, the Japanese people celebrated joyously. The *Japan Times and Advertiser* ran the headline: "U.S. Pacific Fleet Is Wiped Out!" The paper went on to describe the triumphant attack and claimed that Japan had "reduced the U.S. to a third-class power overnight."[20] Tōjō went on the radio to announce the commencement of war with the United States. Afterward, a Japanese choir sang a patriotic song expressing utter joy that across the sea, enemy corpses floated in the water and littered the fields.

In the United States, there was only shock and outrage. One American newspaper reported, "The U.S. Navy was caught with its pants down."[21] And within hours, demands for retaliation issued from every corner of the country. Montana senator Burton K. Wheeler exclaimed, "The only thing to do now is lick the hell out of them!"[22]

On Sunday afternoon President Roosevelt met with his military advisers and members of his cabinet. They immediately began issuing orders for American military installations to receive heavy guard, for all amateur radio operators to be silenced, and for all private planes to be grounded. During the meeting a call came in from Winston Churchill, prime minister of Great Britain. "Mr. President, what's all this about Japan?" Churchill queried. "It's quite true," Roosevelt responded. "They have attacked Pearl Harbor. We are all in the same boat now."[23] Churchill then informed the Americans that the Japanese were at that moment attacking British bases in Malaya. In fact, the assaults on Hawaii and Malaya proved to be only the tip of the iceberg, so to speak. Reports soon poured in that Japan had also attacked the Pacific islands of Guam and Wake as well as British bases in Hong Kong, Singapore, and many other areas in Southeast Asia.

Roosevelt and Churchill agreed to issue simultaneous declarations of war against Japan the next day. Accordingly, at 12:30 P.M. on December 8, Roosevelt stood before a packed joint session of Congress and delivered the American call to arms. His words went out over the radio to millions of Americans and listeners in other countries. "Yesterday," he said,

> December 7, 1941, a date which will live in infamy, the United States was suddenly and deliberately attacked by naval and air forces of the Empire of Japan. . . . It will be recorded that

An aerial photograph of the December 7 attack on Pearl Harbor. President Roosevelt called December 7, 1941, a day that would "live in infamy."

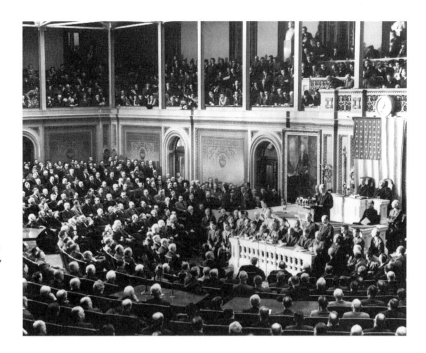

President Roosevelt delivers his famous "Day of Infamy" speech to Congress. In the speech Roosevelt asked for a declaration of war against Japan.

the distance of Hawaii from Japan makes it obvious that the attack was deliberately planned many days or even weeks ago. During the intervening time the Japanese government has deliberately sought to deceive the United States by false statements and expressions of hope for continued peace. . . . Japan has . . . undertaken a surprise offensive extending throughout the Pacific area. . . . As Commander in Chief of the Army and Navy, I have directed that all measures be taken for our defense. . . . No matter how long it may take us to overcome this premeditated invasion, the American people in their righteous might, will win through to absolute victory.[24]

Ending his speech with a dramatic call for a massive war effort against Japan, Roo-

sevelt received a thunderous ovation of clapping and cheers. And without a single word of debate, Congress voted nearly unanimously to declare war.

Within hours all political factions in the country, which usually bickered among themselves, put aside their differences. In a remarkable show of national unity, Americans from all walks of life closed ranks in a show of opposition to the Japanese. Even the famous aviator Charles Lindbergh, a staunch isolationist, lent his support to the war effort, declaring:

> Now it has come, and we must meet it as united Americans regardless of our attitude in the past toward the policy our government has followed. . . . We must now turn every effort to building the greatest and most efficient Army, Navy, and Air Force in the world.[25]

THE REVISIONIST VIEW OF PEARL HARBOR

At the end of World War II, a debate began among politicians, journalists, and historians about the circumstances of the U.S. entry into the war. The official view was that President Roosevelt had done everything in his power to avoid war and was as surprised as everyone else when the Japanese bombed Pearl Harbor.

Some people, however, offered a revised version of the events, saying that Roosevelt and his advisers wanted the Japanese to attack in order to give the United States an excuse for entering the war. Some revisionists said that Roosevelt expected Pearl Harbor to be bombed but purposely refrained from issuing a red alert to U.S. Pacific forces. Writing for the *Wall Street Journal*, William Chamberlain charged, "Like the Roman God Janus, Roosevelt . . . had two faces. . . . For the public record . . . his first concern was to keep the country out of war. But in more intimate surroundings . . . [Roosevelt] assumed that America was already involved in war." According to this view, Roosevelt hoped that wartime industrial production would help the country's economy. Supposedly, he also sought to bolster his own image as a world leader.

But most government officials and historians disagreed with the revisionist view. They stood by the findings of a congressional committee that looked into the matter. The committee found that there was "no evidence to support the charges. . . . On the contrary, all evidence conclusively points to the fact that they [Roosevelt and his advisers] discharged their responsibilities with distinction . . . and in keeping with the highest traditions of our . . . foreign policy."

THE WORLD GOES TO WAR

As war fever spread across the United States, the country's allies, many of them also victims of the Japanese attacks of December 7, declared war on Japan. Winston Churchill told Parliament:

Now that the issue is joined, it only remains for the two great democracies to face their task with whatever strength God may give them. . . . We have at least four-fifths of the population of the globe upon our side. We are responsible for their safety and for their future.[26]

Joining the United States and Britain against Japan were Canada; Australia; New Zealand; the exiled governments of

Greece, Yugoslavia, and France; and nine Latin American countries. These nations referred to themselves as the Allies. Predictably, the other Axis countries, Germany and Italy, backed Japan and declared war on the Allies.

The world was now engulfed in a state of total war. With such a formidable array of nations lined up against Japan, Tōjō and his advisers had little time to assess the implications of their attack on Pearl Harbor. They had assumed that the humiliated Americans would not have the stomach to fight and that the U.S. military threat had been eliminated once and for all. This, however, was a grave miscalculation. The Japanese had indeed dealt the United States a crippling blow at Pearl Harbor; but contrary to what the Japanese hoped and believed, the blow was not a fatal one.

Furthermore, the attackers had made a number of serious mistakes and miscalculations. First, they had failed to bomb the naval repair facilities at Pearl Harbor, so all but two of the damaged ships were quickly refloated and repaired. Second, the Japanese failed to find and destroy the carriers *Lexington* and *Enterprise* and their escort

The failure to find and destroy the American carriers Enterprise *(left) and* Lexington *at Pearl Harbor was a serious mistake on the part of the Japanese.*

ships, which were at sea at the time of the attack. These ships, along with the fighter planes they carried, had the capability of inflicting heavy damage on the Japanese.

Jap? Problems

The most important mistake made by the Japanese leaders was their failure to realize the consequences of drawing the United States into the war. Japan did not realistically take into account the overwhelming industrial might of the U.S. Easy access to vast amounts of oil, coal, metals, and other natural resources essential in waging war meant that the Americans would have a great advantage. The Japanese also failed to anticipate the tremendous food-producing capabilities of the U.S. and neglected to consider the unity and resolve of the American people during a national crisis.

While the Japanese had underestimated the potential power of the United States, Winston Churchill had not. He had been hoping for the two long years his country had been fighting Germany that the Americans would take Britain's side in the war. Churchill knew that once committed to the fighting, the United States would prove to be an incredibly powerful and virtually unstoppable force. Sooner or later, he declared, this force would turn the tide in the battle against the Axis nations. Churchill later wrote:

> No American will think it wrong of me if I proclaim that to have the United States at our side was to me the greatest joy. . . . Hitler's fate was sealed. . . . [Italy's] fate was sealed. As for the Japanese, they would be ground to powder. All the rest was merely the proper application of overwhelming force.[27]

Quote

3 From Batavia to Bataan: The Japanese Empire Expands

At the beginning of the war in the Pacific, Japan enjoyed a brilliant period of expansion during which it encountered little significant resistance from the Allies. This was because the Allies were unprepared to wage a major war against Japan. The United States needed time to rebound from the attack on Pearl Harbor, to gear up its national war production, and to plan its strategy. Meanwhile, Britain and several other European Allies were preoccupied with combating Hitler and needed many more months to mount a second major offensive in the Pacific.

And so the Japanese empire, called the "octopus" by many in the West, reached out to grab several prizes at once. Within days of the assault on the U.S. fleet on Oahu, the Japanese struck at the British colonies of Singapore, Malaya, and Hong Kong in Southeast Asia. Japanese troops poured southward from Indochina into Thailand. And Japanese planes bombed U.S. airfields in the Philippine Islands. At the same time, the Japanese navy took over the American-owned Guam, Wake, and other Pacific islands.

FEARS OF INVASION AND MASS STARVATION

Until such time that the Americans, British, and other Allies could organize a major offensive in the Pacific, locales within that sphere were largely either under Japanese control or in a state of disruption and uncertainty. The most obvious threat to those fighting or not yet under attack by the Japanese was invasion and hostile takeover. Yet numerous other potential dangers existed, not least of which was interruption of food supply and distribution. Islands all across the Pacific, both Japanese- and Allied-held, faced a similar problem; namely, most islands could not produce the huge amounts of food necessary to sustain large armies of soldiers. Much of the food needed by both troops and civilian populations had to be shipped in.

The Japanese could, with considerable difficulty, supply their own bases in the Philippines and elsewhere. More ominously, they could also potentially disrupt, blockade, or otherwise stop food bound for Allied soldiers and civilians. The situation in the Philippines was a case in point. After the Japanese attacked these islands, thousands of American and Filipino fighters resisted the invaders for four months. During that period Japanese warships sank most of the supply ships attempting to get through to the besieged; and the Allied troops suffered severe shortages. Many Allied officials feared the onset of starvation in American-controlled Hawaii as well. As scholars James F. Dunnigan and Albert A. Nofi explain:

> The Hawaiian Islands could not feed themselves. When the Japanese struck on December 7, 1941, the 42,000 U.S. troops in the islands had a sixty-day supply of food. The 420,000 civilians on Oahu were worse off, with less than a forty-day supply. Most of the food consumed on the islands was imported. While the islands contained much fertile land, most had been turned over to plantations growing crops like pineapples. There was a great fear that the Japanese would blockade the islands and starve them into submission, or invade first.[28]

Luckily, no such invasion of Hawaii occurred right away, mainly because it was so far from Japan. Japanese war planners felt their country would be overextending itself to send a huge invasion force such a great distance before it had finished overrunning the Philippines and consolidating other Pacific gains. Once Japan controlled the western and southern Pacific, the thinking went, it could set its sights on Hawaii. As it turned out, this gave the United States the breathing space it needed to ship in needed food and other supplies and begin rebuilding its Pacific Fleet.

THE BRITISH NAVY CRIPPLED

As for Japan's ongoing efforts to secure the main strategic locales of the western Pacific, it was imperative that it confront and cripple the British naval units in the region. Otherwise, the Japanese would have no assurance that they could hold on to the islands they were seizing. One of the most dramatic incidents of Japan's well-coordinated initial offensive, therefore, was its attack on Britain's principal warships in the Far East. Based at Singapore, the 35,000-ton battleship *Prince of Wales* and the 32,000-ton battle cruiser *Repulse* were stationed to protect British colonies in the area. When the Japanese struck locations all over Southeast Asia, British admiral Sir Tom Phillips decided to take the huge vessels to sea and try to destroy Japanese ships in the vicinity. But this proved to be a fatal mistake, for the British ships had no planes to provide protection from the Japanese air force.

On December 9, 1941, two days after the sneak attack on Pearl Harbor, Japanese planes spotted the *Prince of Wales* and the *Repulse* at a distance of about 150 miles from Singapore. According to Japanese war correspondent Yukio Waku:

> Columns of black smoke were sighted far on the horizon. Careful reconnaissance [inspection] told us that the smoke columns were those from

The British ships Repulse *and* Prince of Wales *try to avoid Japanese bombs. The destruction of these two ships left the British with no effective sea power in the Pacific.*

the enemy fleet, which included the *Prince of Wales* and the *Repulse.* . . . Our bombers caught sight of the British Far Eastern Fleet, which seemed to have noticed our attempt and started fleeing in zigzag [movements] at full speed of 30 knots under cover of the dark clouds.[29]

Once located by the Japanese bombers, the British ships, with their lack of air support, were largely defenseless. Wave after wave of attackers swooped in for the kill, dropping their deadly explosives relentlessly and accurately. British correspondent Cecil Brown, who was aboard the *Repulse,* later filed this report describing the end of the two great vessels:

That the *Repulse* was doomed was immediately apparent. The communication system announced: "Prepare to abandon ship. May God be with you!" Without undo rush we all started streaming down ladders, hurrying but not pushing. . . . It seemed so incredible that the *Repulse* could or should go down. But the *Repulse* was fast keeling over to port [the left side] and walking ceased to be a [reliable] mode of locomotion [movement]. . . . Men were lying dead around the guns. . . . There was considerable damage all around the ship. . . . As I go over the side, the *Prince of Wales* half a mile away seems to be afire, but her guns are still firing. . . . Swimming about a mile away, lying on top of a small stool, I saw the bow of the *Wales*. . . . When [it] sank, the suction [of the water] was so great it ripped off the life belt of one officer more than 50 feet away. . . . The gentle, quiet manner in which these shell-belching [battleships] went to their last resting place without exploding was a tribute of gratitude from two fine ships for their fine sailors.[30]

This tragedy shocked the Allies for two reasons. First, the loss of Britain's best warships in the area left most of Southeast Asia defenseless, ensuring that the Japanese would conquer most of the area. As a high-ranking British officer, General Sir Alan Brooke, put it, "It means that from Africa eastward to America through the Indian Ocean and the Pacific, we have lost control of the sea."[31] Second, the incident called into question the effectiveness of large battleships, which had been the mainstay of the world's navies for decades. The sinking of the two giant vessels marked the first time that aircraft alone had sunk ships so large on the open ocean.

Following the elimination of British naval resistance, Japan's leaders grew even more confident. The Japanese octopus continued to reach out on the land and in the air, striking at strategic points in Asia and taking island after island in the Pacific. One key to this entire Japanese offensive was the unusual effectiveness of Japanese fighting men. These troops were highly trained and disciplined. Also, they knew how to survive for extended periods on small rations of rice and could live off the land if necessary. They learned to camouflage themselves to blend in with leaves and underbrush so they could creep unseen through the jungle, and they often used animal cries to signal to one another. Moreover, they were taught to follow the samurai code, choosing to fight to the death rather than surrender. All of these factors made Japanese soldiers extremely fearsome and formidable opponents for American and Allied troops.

THE STRUGGLE FOR THE PHILIPPINES

One of the first major tests for the well-trained Japanese ground fighters was in the Philippines. The Japanese leaders knew that capturing the Philippines, a group of some seventy-one hundred islands controlled by the United States, was essential to winning the war. This was because the Philippines extend for 1,150 miles along the strategic military and

THE ALWAYS CONTROVERSIAL DOUGLAS MACARTHUR

Sometimes called the "American Caesar," Douglas MacArthur (1880–1964) was one of the most important and talked-about leaders of World War II. He graduated first in his class at West Point in 1903 and was wounded and decorated in 1917 during World War I. Appointed to command the U.S. military in the Philippines in 1935, MacArthur gained world attention during the hectic defense of the islands from 1941 to 1942. Later, in 1945, MacArthur accepted the surrender of the Japanese and became the supreme commander for the Allied forces in postwar Japan. He oversaw Japan's rapid reconstruction between 1945 and 1951, then went on to lead the American forces in the Korean War.

Although he sometimes proved himself an excellent strategist, MacArthur was often described by his colleagues as temperamental, ambitious, overly dramatic, and conceited. Believing that his opinions should never be questioned, he regularly argued with his advisers and even his superiors. It was such a disagreement that led President Harry Truman to fire him from his post in Korea in 1951. Always controversial, MacArthur divided the American public into those who hated him because he was power hungry and self-centered and those who loved him as a larger-than-life national hero.

trade routes between Japan and southern Asia. Conquering the Philippines would practically ensure control of the valuable oil and mineral deposits of the Dutch islands of Java and Malaya to the west and the lands of China and Burma to the north.

On December 8, 1941, the Japanese attacked U.S. planes parked on runways at Clark Field, near Manila, the Philippine capital. This and other similar raids destroyed most of the U.S. airpower in the area. In the following three weeks, Japanese troops landed in seven different spots on Luzon, the largest of the Philippine Islands, and quickly drove back the unprepared American defenders. The commander of the American-Filipino forces, General Douglas MacArthur, sent a damage report to Washington on December 27, saying that enemy penetration of the Philippines had resulted from American weakness on the sea and in the air. A lack of airfields for modern planes had permitted unhindered day bombardment, he said, and the enemy had enjoyed complete freedom of naval and air movement.

As the Japanese closed in on Manila, American troops evacuated the city and thousands of Filipinos fled into the hills. Japanese planes then bombed the city, touching off massive fires. A few days later, Japanese troops moved in and took control. Immediately they instituted a code of strict rules that they would later impose on all the peoples they conquered. The code warned:

Anyone who inflicts, or attempts to inflict, an injury upon Japanese soldiers shall be shot to death. If the assailant, or attempted assailant, cannot be found, we will hold ten influential people who are in or about the streets of municipal cities where the event happened.[32]

The iron hand of Japanese colonial rule had begun to tighten its grip on the Philippines.

Seeing no other choice, General MacArthur ordered his troops to retreat to the Bataan Peninsula, in western Luzon, where he hoped they could hold out against the Japanese until help arrived. The Japanese launched massive attacks on Bataan. Cut off from vital food shipments thanks to Japanese destruction of incoming Allied supply ships, the American-Filipino forces ran out of food and had to eat dogs, iguana lizards, monkeys, and snakes, as well as berries and roots from the jungle. Their supplies of medicine also ran out, and they suffered from diseases such as dysentery, malaria, and scurvy. Yet as the weeks dragged by, the demoralized Bataan defenders managed to fight on.

"I Shall Return"

On February 22, 1942, President Roosevelt made a painful decision. He saw that the American

THE PHILIPPINE ISLANDS

LUZON

Manila

Bataan Peninsula

Corregidor

San Bernardino Strait

Sibuyan Sea

SAMAR

Leyte Gulf

Mindanao Sea

Surigao Strait

MINDANAO

BORNEO

Japanese soldiers celebrate their victory in the Philippines. The American surrender there was a triumph for Japan.

situation on Bataan was hopeless and felt it would be disastrous for the morale of the United States and Allies if General MacArthur, one of their most popular generals and public figures, fell into enemy hands. Roosevelt ordered a special group of commandos to evacuate MacArthur and his family in secrecy to Australia. Before leaving, MacArthur told General Jonathan M. Wainwright, who now took charge of the U.S. forces, to defend Bataan as best as he could. If surrender became necessary, MacArthur emphasized, Wainwright must destroy as many American weapons as he could so that they could not be used against an American effort to recapture the Philippines. "If I get through to Australia," said MacArthur, "you know I'll come back as soon as I can with as much as I can. In the meantime, you've got to hold."[33]

Indeed, the retaking of the Philippines became not only a major U.S. goal of the war, but also one of MacArthur's chief personal goals and responsibilities. When he arrived in Australia, he told the world, "The President . . . ordered me to break through the Japanese lines . . . for the purpose . . . of organizing the American offensive against Japan, a primary purpose of which is the relief of the Philippines." In a stirring ending to the speech, MacArthur vowed to the people of the Philippines, "I shall return!"[34]

SURRENDER OF THE PHILIPPINES AND ITS IMPACT

Unfortunately, despite heroic efforts, Wainwright and his men were unable to withstand the Japanese onslaught. On April 9, 1942, thirty-six thousand Americans and several thousand Filipinos on Bataan surrendered. Thousands of others managed to escape to Corregidor, a tiny island off the Luzon coast. The captured soldiers at Bataan were forced on a bloody death march to prison camps in northern Luzon. Meanwhile, the fifteen thousand Americans on Corregidor, heavily bombarded by Japanese artillery and torpedoes, were able to hold out until May 6, when they too were forced to surrender.

The conquest of the Philippines was a major triumph for the Japanese empire. For one thing, the loss of the islands was a massive and humiliating defeat for the Allies. More importantly, the Japanese now had Manila Harbor, one of the finest in the world, which they could use to supply their bases in Burma and Java. Moreover, the newly established Japanese bases in the Philippines could be used to launch attacks against the Allies all over Southeast Asia. Eventually, the Japanese hoped, the Philippines would become the staging area for an invasion of Australia.

Many Americans, as well as British and other Allies, wondered how a country as strong as the United States could lose a holding as important strategically as the Philippines. Quite naturally, such inquiry inevitably focused on the man who had had charge of the islands—Douglas MacArthur. Though MacArthur was undoubtedly one of the most capable military leaders the United States had at the time, his failure to prepare for and fend off the Japanese attack was and remains controversial. "Despite ample warning of a Japanese attack," Dunnigan and Nofi write,

> nearly a half day after Pearl Harbor MacArthur allowed his air force to be largely destroyed on the ground. Although the Japanese air bases were [only] 500 miles away, MacArthur did not order his aircraft dispersed, nor did he take pains to resist the Japanese air attacks effectively. Similar errors were made with the ground forces. Although MacArthur had been in the Philippines for several years, he failed to take into account the low training levels of his Philippine troops when reacting to the actual Japanese invasion. . . . When the Japanese invaded, MacArthur decided to try to

THE BATAAN DEATH MARCH

When the American-Filipino garrison on Bataan surrendered in April 1942, the Japanese decided to march the seventy-six thousand prisoners to holding camps farther north. The treatment of the prisoners by their captors was one of the most shocking examples of senseless and inhuman brutality in the annals of warfare. On April 11 the Japanese tied hundreds of Filipino officers to poles and mercilessly bayoneted them to death. Herded into columns, the Americans and other Filipinos had to march without water under the blazing tropical sun. Japanese guards beat the men with rifle butts as they walked; and those who fell and could not get up were bayoneted. Some had to dig their own graves, and when they were done, guards buried them alive. Guards also taunted the prisoners with food and water but never gave them any. Even men sick with malaria or hobbling on crutches were tortured and brutalized. After six terrible days, the ragtag column reached the camps. More than twenty-two thousand prisoners had died on the march, and thousands more perished from disease and lack of food in the following months.

American prisoners march toward northern holding camps. Twenty-two thousand Americans died on the march.

halt the Japanese in mobile operations on the North Luzon Plain. The results were disastrous. The American and Filipino troops fought bravely . . . and actually managed to slow the Japanese advance. But in the process, many of MacArthur's handful of experienced men and much of the best equipment were lost. Meanwhile, troops and supply movements were bungled before and during the land battles. . . . Overall, MacArthur performed in a decidedly lackluster manner, especially compared to his later accomplishments.[35]

Though some felt that MacArthur was to blame for the debacle and should be fired outright, a number of factors worked in his favor and saved him from disgrace. First, he had a towering reputation as a military leader, having distinguished himself during World War I. Second, many Americans took him at his

General Douglas MacArthur was criticized for failing to prepare for and fend off the Japanese attack on the Philippines.

word when he skillfully argued that he had done the best anyone could be expected to do under such dire circumstances. And third, leaders in Washington needed a hero who was well known in the Pacific area for the American and Filipino forces to rally around. As a result, MacArthur emerged from the defeat in one piece and began preparing for a rematch with the Japanese who had ousted him. Whatever the American leaders and public may have thought about MacArthur's conduct and evacuation to Australia, a good many of his former troops were resentful. They remembered him as "Dugout Doug," who had spent much of his time in a dugout (a concrete bunker) and then fled to safety while they bore the brunt of the invasion.

JAPAN AT ITS ZENITH

Many other strategic locales fell to Japan's overwhelming 1942 offensive. On February 27, 1942, the Japanese destroyed an entire fleet of American, British, and Dutch ships off the coast of Java and then invaded the island. By March 9 the attackers had taken control of the former Dutch colony, including its capital of Batavia, and had captured ninety-eight thousand Allied prisoners. Then, after many weeks of bloody fighting, Burma, on the Asian mainland, fell to the Japanese in May 1942. Java and Burma were important prizes for Japan because they contained rich supplies of oil, rubber, metal ores, and foodstuffs. But the greatest prize of all would be Australia, the continent in

the southern Pacific covering almost 3 million square miles. Taking Australia, the Japanese believed, would completely demoralize the Allies. And then no one would be able to dislodge Japan from its new Pacific empire.

As Japan's naval, air, and land forces ran wild in the Pacific, the United States could do little to check enemy advances. The Americans did engage the Japanese in a naval battle in the Coral Sea, north of Australia, in May 1942, but there were nearly equal losses on both sides. Apart from delaying the Japanese invasion of Australia, the confrontation was largely indecisive. By mid-1942, to the dismay of the Allies, the Japanese empire was at the height of its power.

The only moment of triumph for the United States in the early days of the war came in April 1942, when Colonel James Doolittle led a brief bombing raid over Tokyo, Japan's capital and largest city. The operation had no significant strategic value, but rather was designed mainly to boost the morale of the American troops and public. Doolittle's force consisted of sixteen B-25 bombers carrying a total of eighty pilots and other personnel. The aircraft carrier *Hornet*, accompanied by several support vessels, ferried the planes to a point about 650 miles from Japan. From there, the bombers took off for their historic mission. Ronald Spector provides this summary of its effects:

> In Tokyo, the Japanese were just completing an air-raid drill when the first American planes appeared. Sweeping in on the city at treetop level, the first

DESTROY YAMAMOTO AT ALL COSTS

Isoroku Yamamoto (1884–1943), commander in chief of the Japanese navy at the onset of the Pacific War and one of the most brilliant military leaders of World War II, grew up hating the United States. His father had told him bedtime stories about "the barbarians who came in their black ships" in the 1800s, "broke down the doors of Japan, threatened the Son of Heaven, and trampled the ancient customs."

To learn his enemy's weaknesses, Yamamoto traveled to the United States in the 1920s and studied at Harvard University. He quickly gained a healthy respect for the vast potential of American industrial and military might. This convinced him that fighting a conventional war with the United States and its allies would be a catastrophic mistake for Japan. When called on to serve his country, therefore, he came up with the idea for the attack on Pearl Harbor, seeing it as the only way to eliminate American naval superiority.

Rightly viewing Yamamoto as one of Japan's most important military assets, American military officials wanted to eliminate him; but for a

long time they were unable to find him. Finally, on April 18, 1943, radio operators intercepted a secret message pinpointing the exact location of Yamamoto's personal plane. Ordered that they "must at all costs reach and destroy Yamamoto and his staff," sixteen U.S. planes attacked the admiral the next morning. In a matter of minutes, the Americans completed their mission, robbing the Japanese of their best strategist.

Isoroku Yamamoto masterminded the attack on Pearl Harbor because he believed that fighting a conventional war with the United States would prove catastrophic for Japan.

One of Colonel James Doolittle's B-25s takes off from the carrier Hornet. *Doolittle's raid on Japan had no significant strategic value but was designed to boost American morale.*

two bombers released their bomb loads and swung away unscathed. Twenty minutes later, the remaining planes reached the city; they met occasionally heavy but inaccurate antiaircraft fire. . . . [After the raid] fifteen of the sixteen planes managed to reach China. With their fuel exhausted, they crash-landed or were abandoned in the air by their crews. . . . Of the eighty men . . . seventy-one survived. The damage inflicted by the raid was small, but its psychological effect on the Japanese was all that might have

been desired. The [Japanese] army and navy had failed in their duty to safeguard the homeland and the Emperor from attack. Admiral Yamamoto regarded the raid as a mortifying personal defeat.[36]

Because the Doolittle raid was such a humiliating stain on their country's honor, the Japanese militarists vowed to retaliate by destroying the remainder of the U.S. fleet. Yamamoto, who had long advocated the strategic importance of taking the Hawaiian Islands, engineered a plan to lure the Americans into a trap. If it worked, the U.S. West Coast would be left unguarded. He and other Japanese leaders reasoned that a weakened and frightened America would then desire peace on any terms that Japan might dictate. Accordingly, Japanese admirals began to assemble the largest naval operation in Japanese history. Their target was Midway Island, at the far western tip of the Hawaiian chain. Yamamoto envisioned correctly that this engagement would prove to be a major turning point for Japan; but as history has shown, its outcome would be quite different than he had imagined.

Chapter

4 Turning Point at Midway: The United States Strikes Back

In May 1942 the Japanese empire was enjoying its greatest expansion, while the Americans were still attempting to recover from the disaster at Pearl Harbor. Each side knew that its number-one priority must be to formulate an overall offensive strategy, a plan of attack against the other country. In creating such strategy, each side tried to guess the other's intentions, while military planners also took into consideration matters of national security and self-defense.

For instance, the Japanese strategy changed significantly in response to the Doolittle raid. Before the American strike on Tokyo in April, Japanese leaders were convinced that their country was well protected, that no American planes would ever be able to penetrate Japan's defenses and threaten the homeland. But the successful Doolittle mission showed the Japanese that their country was indeed exposed to destruction from the air. In particular, the life of Emperor Hirohito was at risk. This single fact so terrified Japanese leaders that they vowed to increase the country's level of security.

Never again, they said, would the American "barbarians" break through and bomb Japanese cities.

To war strategists in Tokyo, one dangerous hole in the Japanese defenses was Midway Island, at the tip of the Hawaiian Islands, about eleven hundred miles west of Oahu. Though only six miles in diameter, Midway was a key point in the American line of defense and a gateway to the other Hawaiian Islands. Admiral Yamamoto and his staff formulated strategy for a huge-scale attack on Midway. They hoped this move would destroy the remainder of the American fleet and eventually lead to Japanese control of the entire Hawaiian chain. Then, they reasoned, the United States would have no significant beachhead left in the Pacific region and be virtually eliminated from the war.

CRACKING THE JAPANESE CODE

Conversely, the Americans fully realized the strategic importance of controlling

JAPANESE PROPAGANDA FILMS

By the 1930s, film was a highly popular and influential form of mass communication. Millions of people around the world went to the movies on a regular basis, and the stories presented on the screen helped shape the way people saw their world. Naturally, government and military leaders of many nations were quick to use the cinema to mold public opinion. Propaganda films became a powerful weapon in the hands of moviemakers in the United States, Britain, Germany, Japan, and other countries.

In the late 1930s, as Japan invaded China and threatened other areas of Southeast Asia, Japanese war films tended to emphasize personal stories of individual heroes. For instance, *Five Scouts* (1938), directed by Tomotaka Tasaka, depicted the trials of five young soldiers fighting in northern China. The style of the film was sentimental, focusing on the men's memories of home and family rather than glorifying war itself. Tasaka's *Mud and Soldiers* (1939) and Kimisaburo Yoshimura's *The Story of Tank Commander Nischizumi* (1940), also set in China, showed Japanese soldiers helping rather than exploiting the Chinese peasants.

In 1940 the Japanese government set up the Office of Public Information specifically to produce propaganda films. And the tone of Japanese movies changed drastically. The films began to emphasize themes such as national loyalty and the invincibility of Japan. Most included long sequences of guns firing, soldiers marching, or bombs exploding, often accompanied by powerful classical music and heavenly choirs. *Capture of Burma, The War at Sea from Hawaii to Malaya,* and *The Suicide Troops of the Watchtower* (all 1942) were typical examples.

the Hawaiian Islands and worked around the clock to rebuild their defenses there. Just as important, they knew, too, that they desperately needed a major victory. Somehow they must deliver a damaging blow to the Japanese navy, both to even the odds after the devastating losses at Pearl Harbor and to lift the morale of the American people and the Allies.

But American leaders also realized that the Japanese now controlled most of the Pacific. Japanese ships moved constantly, swiftly, and largely unchallenged from one strategic point to another. To have a chance at victory, the

Americans had to be able to track Japanese ship movements and know their plans. To discover this information, the United States needed to break the Japanese secret military code.

Immediately after the attack on Pearl Harbor, a group of American cryptologists (experts at making and breaking complicated codes) set to work to crack the Japanese code. The group had its own secret code name—Hypo. Since the war had begun, John Costello explains, the Hypo team

> had been battling night and day to penetrate the five-digit groups of the Japanese Navy's main operational code, which had been labeled JN (Japanese Navy) No. 25. . . . It was a process requiring painstaking skill and intuition on the part of the decrypting teams, multiple filing systems, and batteries of IBM tabulating machines [primitive forms of today's computers] fed with stacks of punch cards. . . . The JN25 code . . . was a traditional cipher generated from two code books. There was a "dictionary" volume containing columns of 45,000 randomly selected five-digit groups such as 43752, 65739 [and so forth]. Each set was ascribed to a particular word . . . in "Kama"—the phonetic version of the Japanese ideograms [picture signs]—into which the message was translated. Before transmission, each group was added to successive similar five-digit groups from a second book.[37]

To maintain high security, Japanese naval officers had intended to replace the two codebooks on April 1. But they became overconfident, believing that their code was too clever for the "inferior" American experts to decipher; so the Japanese postponed the update until June.

This gave the American cryptologists the time they needed to break the code. By early April 1942, the Hypo experts were able to read 15 percent of the messages intercepted from the Japanese. Applying that knowledge to other portions of the enemy code, the Americans could decipher 85 percent of the messages by early May. A few messages still could not be decoded, but the Hypo team members felt confident that they could make educated guesses about what they did not know.

A dramatic test for the Hypo unit came only days later. On May 12 the Americans decoded messages indicating that the Japanese would strike soon at the Hawaiian Islands. The messages referred to the target as "AF." But no one could figure out where AF was. So Hypo captain Jasper Holmes devised a simple but ingenious way to find out. He had the American base on Midway send out an uncoded message, a complaint that the base's water-purification plant had broken down. Within two days, Japanese signals flashed across the Pacific saying that AF had problems with its water.

Holmes's trick had worked, and the Americans now knew for sure that Midway would be the target. Furthermore, on May 20 other intercepted Japanese messages indicated the date and time of the attack. The

Japanese would strike Alaska's Aleutian Islands on June 3 to confuse and divert the attention of the Americans, then assault Midway the next day. Unknown to the Japanese, the Americans secretly began preparing their own forces for the coming battle.

CRUCIAL DIFFERENCES IN NAVAL STRATEGY

The showdown between the Americans and Japanese at Midway was one of the most important and decisive naval battles in history. The Japanese assembled a

AMERICAN PROPAGANDA FILMS

In the United States, which was the world's largest producer of motion pictures, the output of war propaganda films was predictably heavy. Before the 1941 attack on Pearl Harbor, nearly all of the American war films depicted the fighting in Europe, showing the German and Italian dictators as cruel and corrupt.

After the United States went to war with Japan, anti-Japanese films appeared in two forms. First, there were highly polished documentary-style films that showed real news and battle footage and explained why it was important to defeat the enemy. The best and most famous of these were the *Why We Fight* films, directed by the famous Hollywood filmmaker Frank Capra, who headed the U.S. War Department Film Section at the time. Another Hollywood director, John Ford, made the powerful documentary films *The Battle of Midway* (1942) and *December 7th* (1943).

The other kind of American propaganda film was the full-length Hollywood film, designed to entertain but also to arouse patriotism and build morale. *Bataan* (1943), with Robert Taylor, depicted the American defense of the Bataan Peninsula, as did *So Proudly We Hail* (1943), with Claudette Colbert. *Guadalcanal Diary* (1943), based on the actual eyewitness accounts of Richard Tregaskis, told the stirring tale of Americans caught in the bloody jungle fighting north of Australia. Exploiting this film's propaganda potential, the War Department set up recruiting stations near theaters where it showed. Among the other notable patriotic American films of the war were *Thirty Seconds Over Tokyo* (1944), the story of the dramatic Doolittle raid, starring Spencer Tracy; and *They Were Expendable* (1945), about the heroic service of the small torpedo boats based in the Philippines, starring John Wayne.

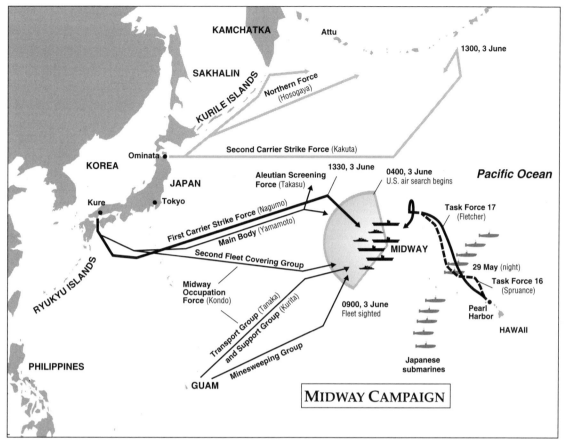

Map labels:
KAMCHATKA
Attu
1300, 3 June
SAKHALIN
Northern Force (Hosogaya)
KURILE ISLANDS
Second Carrier Strike Force (Kakuta)
Ominata
KOREA
1330, 3 June
0400, 3 June U.S. air search begins
Pacific Ocean
Aleutian Screening Force (Takasu)
JAPAN
Task Force 17 (Fletcher)
Kure
Tokyo
First Carrier Strike Force (Nagumo)
Main Body (Yamamoto)
Second Fleet Covering Group
MIDWAY
29 May (night)
Task Force 16 (Spruance)
RYUKYU ISLANDS
Midway Occupation Force (Kondo)
Transport Group (Tanaka) and Support Group (Kurita)
0900, 3 June Fleet sighted
Pearl Harbor
HAWAII
PHILIPPINES
Minesweeping Group
Japanese submarines
GUAM
MIDWAY CAMPAIGN

gigantic fleet of more than 200 ships, including 11 battleships, 8 aircraft carriers, and 21 submarines. The carriers held more than 700 deadly fighter planes and bombers. By contrast, the Americans had only 70 ships, 3 of which were carriers, and about 350 planes, including those stationed on Midway itself.

Despite their numerical superiority in ships and planes, the Japanese made three serious errors. First, they expected the Americans to be surprised and unprepared. If the Americans had not known an attack was coming at Midway, their forces would have been too far away to stop the invasion. The Japanese did not realize that the Americans had broken their code and therefore knew when and where the attack would come.

The second mistake the Japanese made was dividing their fleet into five separate units. These units were spread out over an area of several thousand square miles, which, some worried Japanese naval officers pointed out, would make it difficult for the units to come to one another's aid. But these officers were overruled. Their superiors declared that each unit had a group of battleships and destroyers to protect its carriers from attack by American ships. If the Americans found and engaged one unit, the reasoning went, the other four units could still take Midway and threaten Hawaii.

The third flaw in the Japanese plan was the assumption that the main American counterattack, if any, would come from battleships. This proved to be one of the gravest miscalculations of modern warfare. The commander of the U.S. fleet, Admiral Chester W. Nimitz, believed, quite rightly it turned out, that traditional naval strategy centering around battleships had become outdated. Carrying on the traditions established by European warships in prior centuries, the huge vessels normally moved close to an enemy fleet and blasted away with their big guns. But battleships presented easy targets for dive-bombers; and unlike aircraft carriers, they could not carry planes. Nimitz ordered American battleships to remain on the U.S. West Coast and built his plans around aircraft carriers. He would rely on his warplanes stationed on these carriers to strike quickly and cover great distances.

A DEADLY SERIES OF DELAYS

At 4:30 A.M. on the morning of June 4, 1942, the unsuspecting Japanese launched their attack on Midway as planned. Taking off from the carriers *Akagi, Kaga,*

The Japanese carrier Kaga *was one of four carriers the Japanese used to launch their attack on Midway.*

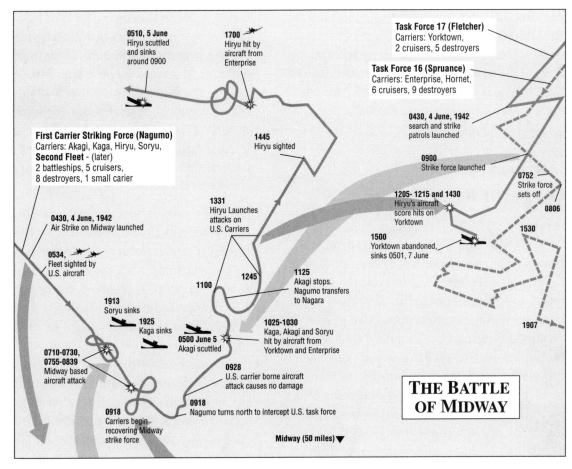

0510, 5 June
Hiryu scuttled and sinks around 0900

1700
Hiryu hit by aircraft from Enterprise

Task Force 17 (Fletcher)
Carriers: Yorktown, 2 cruisers, 5 destroyers

Task Force 16 (Spruance)
Carriers: Enterprise, Hornet, 6 cruisers, 9 destroyers

0430, 4 June, 1942
search and strike patrols launched

0900
Strike force launched

0752
Strike force sets off

First Carrier Striking Force (Nagumo)
Carriers: Akagi, Kaga, Hiryu, Soryu,
Second Fleet - (later)
2 battleships, 5 cruisers,
8 destroyers, 1 small carier

1445
Hiryu sighted

0806

1331
Hiryu Launches attacks on U.S. Carriers

1205- 1215 and 1430
Hiryu's aircraft score hits on Yorktown

0430, 4 June, 1942
Air Strike on Midway launched

1500
Yorktown abandoned, sinks 0501, 7 June

1530

0534,
Fleet sighted by U.S. aircraft

1100

1245

1125
Akagi stops. Nagumo transfers to Nagara

1913
Soryu sinks

1925
Kaga sinks

0500 June 5
Akagi scuttled

1025-1030
Kaga, Akagi and Soryu hit by aircraft from Yorktown and Enterprise

1907

0710-0730,
0755-0839
Midway based aircraft attack

0928
U.S. carrier borne aircraft attack causes no damage

THE BATTLE OF MIDWAY

0918
Carriers begin recovering Midway strike force

0918
Nagumo turns north to intercept U.S. task force

Midway (50 miles) ▼

Hiryu, and *Soryu,* in the main force commanded by Admiral Nagumo, 108 planes assaulted the island's air base. Because the Americans knew the attack was coming, the base's planes made it into the air quickly and launched a counterstrike on Nagumo's ships. The planes did little damage but convinced Nagumo that he needed to launch a second strike against the Midway base in order to wipe out American resistance. Accordingly, he ordered another wave of bombers to be fitted with torpedoes for the attack.

Only a few hours later, at 7:30 A.M., Japanese planes spotted ten American warships just two hundred miles from Nagumo's fleet. Confused now about whether he should attack the island or the U.S. ships, the Japanese admiral hesitated. He waited to find out if the American fleet included an aircraft carrier, sending his spotter pilots the message "Ascertain ship types and maintain contact."[38] It was 8:20 before a Japanese pilot reported, "The enemy is accompanied by what appears to be a carrier bringing up the rear."[39] Knowing the danger posed by a carrier's planes, Nagumo decided to attack the ships.

At that moment, however, the Japanese planes that had struck Midway returned, needing to land on Nagumo's carriers. And his second wave of bombers was still waiting on deck to be fitted with torpedoes. This forced Nagumo to make further delays, the sum total of which proved to be fatal for the Japanese fleet.

U.S. Planes Move
In for the Kill

While Nagumo hesitated, U.S. Lieutenant C.W. McClusky, leading a squadron of planes from the carrier *Enterprise*, spotted Nagumo's carriers. McClusky spread the word to the Americans. In less than an hour, wave after wave of American planes swooped down on the Japanese fleet. For the Japanese, this was the worst possible moment for an attack. Almost one hundred planes, still waiting to take off to bomb the Americans, lined the decks of the carriers. Each plane was loaded with bombs, torpedoes, and flammable fuel. Also stacked on the carrier decks were piles of torpedoes and other explosives.

As the American planes dive-bombed their targets, they touched off massive chain reactions of explosions, which turned the ships into floating torches. Mitsuo Fuchida, leader of the attack on Pearl Harbor, was aboard the *Akagi* (recuperating from a bout of appendicitis) and later recalled:

> The terrifying scream of the dive-bombers reached me first, followed by the crashing explosion of a direct hit. There was a blinding flash and then a second explosion, much louder than

the first. I was shaken by a weird blast of warm air. . . . I was horrified at the destruction that had been wrought in a matter of seconds. There was a huge hole in the flight deck. . . . Deck plates reeled upward in grotesque configurations. Planes stood tail up, belching livid flame and jet-black smoke. Reluctant tears streamed down my cheeks as I watched the fires spread.[40]

While the American planes rained deadly bombs on Nagumo's ships, the American carriers *Hornet, Yorktown,* and *Enterprise* sent out still more waves of aircraft. They scored repeated, devastating hits on the Japanese battleships and cruisers, which circled in a state of desperate confusion.

Hearing of the destruction of Nagumo's task force, Admiral Yamamoto called off the invasion and ordered the other four Japanese naval units to retreat. The entire U.S. fleet chased the enemy westward for more than two days, picking off more ships and planes. In the chaos of the retreat, two Japanese ships collided, after which American planes moved in, sank one of the vessels, and badly damaged the other. When the Americans finally broke off the chase, what was left of the Japanese fleet limped slowly away toward a humiliating homecoming in Japan.

The Strategic
Importance of Midway

The encounter at Midway marked the first great turning point of the Pacific War.

An American destroyer comes to the aid of the USS Yorktown. *The* Yorktown *was the only carrier the United States lost during the Battle of Midway.*

"Pearl Harbor has now been partially avenged," remarked Nimitz following the battle. But "vengeance will not be complete until Japanese sea power is reduced to impotence."[41] Nimitz and his officers received a torrent of congratulations from American and Allied leaders and ordinary citizens alike, and for good reason. It was the first decisive defeat the Japanese navy had suffered in 350 years. Japan lost more than 5,000 men, 4 aircraft carriers, several other ships, and 322 planes. American losses were much smaller: 307 men, 1 carrier (the *Yorktown*), and 147 planes.

The overwhelming American victory did more than inflict heavy losses on the enemy, however. Forced to reshuffle their forces in the Pacific, the Japanese had to cancel their plans to invade Australia, New Zealand, and other key Pacific targets. Moreover, the defeat of the Japanese fleet ended all threats to the U.S. West Coast. It also put Japan on the defensive, as henceforth its forces would be increasingly confined to the southern Pacific and their own home waters.

In addition, the clash at Midway proved that Nimitz had been right about the potential of naval airpower. The battle once and for all marked the end of traditional naval strategy centered around battleships with large guns. Surprisingly, the

Navy Chief Chester Nimitz

As commander in chief of the U.S. Pacific Fleet, Chester W. Nimitz (1885–1966) led his country's naval forces from the defeat at Pearl Harbor in 1941 to total victory over Japan in 1945. After attending the U.S. Naval Academy at Annapolis, Maryland, he served on submarines during World War I. In 1939 he headed the navy's Bureau of Navigation, taking on the role of commander in chief after the attack on Pearl Harbor.

Nimitz was known for his organizational abilities and calm manner in times of danger. He oversaw the team of admirals that won the battles of Midway (1942), the Solomon Islands (1942–1943), the Marshall Islands and the Philippines (1944), and Iwo Jima (1945). He correctly foresaw the end of traditional battleship strategy and recognized the importance of naval airpower. Noted historian Samuel E. Morrison said of Nimitz, "He had the capacity to organize . . . the leadership to weld his own subordinates into a great fighting team, the courage to take necessary risks, and the wisdom to select . . . the correct strategy to defeat Japan."

Japanese had not learned a lesson from their own earlier success—when the British warships *Prince of Wales* and *Repulse* had been helpless under Japanese air attack—that the key to modern war was airpower. In fact, none of the big warships at Midway exchanged fire; instead, the planes did all the fighting. In the future, all naval operations would be planned around aircraft carriers.

America Imprisons Its Own Citizens

Just as U.S. Pacific forces had mobilized to meet the Japanese at Midway, Americans at home marshaled their human and material resources for the war effort. One of the first concerns of this mobilization was to ensure that national security was not threatened. Many in the United States expressed what turned out to be an unreasonable fear, namely, that Americans of Japanese ancestry, or AJAs, would become spies or otherwise commit treason against the country. Giving in to this fear, the federal government ordered that Japanese Americans be forcibly removed from their homes and taken to internment camps in central California, Nevada, and Utah. The government confiscated their property and businesses, and the operation cruelly broke up many families. Some people ended up dying in the camps as well.

Those who supported the internment agreed with hysterical law enforcement officials who met in California in January 1942. According to historian Roger V. Daniels, the Los Angeles district attorney

asserted that the U.S. Supreme Court [whose members opposed such in-

A notice posted in San Francisco on April 1, 1942, gives instructions on evacuation procedures for Japanese residents ordered to internment camps.

ternment] was packed with leftist and other extreme advocates of civil liberty and that it was time for the people of California to disregard the law if necessary to secure their protection. . . . One high official was heard to state that he favored shooting on sight all Japanese residents of the state.[42]

These men were not alone. Many Americans agreed with popular newspaper columnist Henry McLemore when he wrote:

I am for the immediate removal of every Japanese on the West Coast to a point deep in the interior. . . . Herd 'em up, pack 'em off and give them the inside room in the Badlands. Let 'em be pinched, hurt, hungry and dead up against it. . . . Let us have no patience with the enemy or with anyone whose veins carry his blood.[43]

Those against the action called it the most blatant mass violation of civil liberties in American history. They insisted that the internment was really motivated by ignorance and racism. The United States was also at war with Germany and Italy, they pointed out, but no Americans of German or Italian descent had been interned.

In fact, the action turned out to be both pointless and embarrassing for the country. Many AJAs fought in the U.S. Army during the war, serving the nation with great distinction and proving their loyalty. And many years after the war, some of the people who had been interned or had relatives die in the camps successfully sued the government.[44]

Japanese Americans arrive at California's Santa Anita detention camp on April 5, 1942. Japanese internment proved both pointless and embarrassing for the United States.

THE AMAZING U.S. AND ALLIED MOBILIZATION

As for the more just and concrete aspects of mobilization, to boost the country's war economy, President Roosevelt and Congress instituted several important measures. First, on December 27, 1941, they set up a system of rationing. This meant that civilians could buy only limited amounts of many products, such as tires, gasoline, shoes, sugar, coffee, and

meat. Rationing allowed more of these items to be shipped to soldiers in Europe and the Pacific.

The war mobilization created more than material shortages in the United States. Sending millions of American men overseas created a huge labor shortage as well. To compensate, millions of women, most of whom had never before worked full-time outside the home, filled many of the vacant jobs in industry and business. Noted painter Norman Rockwell popularized the tough, capable, and proud Rosie the Riveter, who became a symbol of American women doing their part to help win the war. At the peak of wartime employment, almost 19 million women of all ages worked at least twenty-five hours a week; and most of them put in well over forty hours a week. Also, more than 100,000 women served in the armed forces, including some 5,000 in administrative jobs in the Pacific theater. (The outstanding performance of women in both industry and the military during the war became an important factor in changing social attitudes about women, leading to

"Rosey the Riveter" became a symbol of American women helping to win the war.

their increased acceptance in the workplace in the postwar years.)

In addition, on February 9, 1943, Roosevelt mandated a forty-eight-hour workweek, eight hours more than in prewar days. A few months later, on June 25, Congress made labor strikes illegal in government-controlled plants. Both of these measures ensured that the output of war materials would not slow down. That output was the most important aspect of the U.S. war mobilization. In 1942 in order to meet the threat from the Japanese in the Pacific, as well as from the other Axis nations in Europe, the United States embarked upon the greatest war production effort the world had ever seen. In an awesome display of industrial planning and production, tens of thousands of factories employing millions of workers operated twenty-four hours a day, seven days a week. The plants turned out tremendous quantities of weapons, clothes, food, and many other products.

Even more amazing was the speed with which American industry organized and expanded. Only one year after the bombing of Pearl Harbor, U.S. war production already equaled the entire industrial output of Japan, Germany, and Italy combined. And by 1943 production in the United States far surpassed that of the Axis countries.

Indeed, the amount of materials the wartime United States produced was truly staggering. The country became the world's leading shipbuilding nation overnight. Reducing the amount of time needed to build a ship from thirty to seven weeks, and turning out ship parts on huge assembly lines, American workers produced thousands of vessels a year. Between 1942 and 1945, the United States turned out 296,601 planes, 87,000 tanks, over 2.4 million trucks, and 17.4 million rifles. In addition, American farms produced hundreds of millions of tons of beef, chicken, potatoes, dairy products, grains, and other foodstuffs for the country, its soldiers, and its allies. (A large proportion of the total goods turned out went to Great Britain, the Soviet Union, and other countries fighting with the United States against the Axis powers.) In the words of historian Louis L. Snyder, "The Axis was literally engulfed under a sea of American war production."[45]

DISMEMBERING THE OCTOPUS

Following the U.S. victory at Midway, the mounting flood of ships, planes, guns, and other armaments produced by American factories began to pour into the Pacific. In the face of mounting Allied strength, Japanese forces in the Pacific had no choice but to go on the defensive. Meanwhile, the United States wasted no time in following up its victory at Midway. While convoying masses of war materials across the ocean, the Americans attacked the Japanese at the island of Guadalcanal, several hundred miles northeast of Australia, in August 1942. The fighting on Guadalcanal lasted six months, and the battles there on land, sea,

In August, 1942 American forces landed on Guadalcanal and began a six-month-long campaign to take the island.

and in the air were fierce and bloody. Noted historian Samuel E. Morison, who took part in the struggle, recalled the "desperate fights in the air, furious night naval battles, frantic work at supply and construction, savage fighting in the sodden jungles, nights broken by screaming bombs and deafening explosions of naval shells."[46] By February 1943 the Americans, supported by heroic actions from the Australians, had managed to drive the Japanese from the islands directly north of Australia. The Japanese threat to the "land down under" was over.

American leaders now saw the overall strategy they must use to win the war against Japan. Using its military and industrial might, the United States would bombard the enemy in wave after punishing wave. Fighting to take back each of the conquered islands and territories, the Americans would chop off the tentacles of the Japanese octopus one by one. The U.S. forces would relentlessly apply pressure, shove, outshoot, outrun, outmaneuver, and where possible obliterate the enemy, never stopping until they reached the very shores of the Japanese home islands.

Chapter

5 "In Death There Is Life": Japan's Desperate Defensive

As the United States relentlessly pushed the enemy westward toward their homeland, the Japanese forces desperately fought to hold their ground. But the Americans, aided by the British, Australians, and other Allied forces, steadily and methodically retook the Japanese-held islands and territories of the Pacific and Southeast Asia. The Allied onslaught demonstrated the ultimate vulnerability and failure of Japan's overall strategy in both its bid for global power and its self-defense. That strategy, James Dunnigan and Albert Nofi point out,

> was to seize as many islands as possible and fortify enough of them with so many ground troops and aircraft that the Allies would not be able to get through to Japan. It didn't work. The keystone of Japanese strategy was economic resources. The Japanese islands had few natural resources and nearly all the raw materials for Japanese industry had to be imported. While China and Korea provided sufficient ores and food, the oil had to come from fields in Indonesia. It was to obtain access to this oil that Japan went to war with the United States,

Great Britain, and the Netherlands. Japan's strategy was one of desperation, as the Indonesian oil fields could not produce sufficient oil for Japanese needs. More to the point, Japan could not produce sufficient tankers to get the oil from Indonesia to Japan. Allied submarines kept sinking Japanese tankers, and shipping in general. Many senior Japanese military leaders recognized the futility of the war but they carried out their orders anyway. Death before dishonor was more than just a catchphrase in the Japanese military.[47]

Indeed, death before dishonor increasingly became a defining feature of the desperate defensive actions waged by Japanese soldiers in the Pacific sphere. Facing increasingly overwhelming odds, many of these soldiers turned to the ancient samurai code to save their honor. Believing that dying in battle guaranteed them a place in heaven, they often charged fearlessly at American machine guns and artillery. And when it came to a final decision between death and surrender, thousands of Japanese chose death. It must be emphasized that they were partly spurred on by propaganda issued by the Japanese government, which claimed that Americans were merciless barbarians who would destroy the Japanese home islands, rape Japanese women, and slaughter prisoners of war.

American soldiers found Japanese ideas about honor and death bizarre and, not surprisingly, often looked upon the enemy as having little respect for life. This image was reinforced by reports that the Japanese treated Allied prisoners of war inhumanely. Every American knew about the brutal Bataan death march and had heard stories of Japanese interrogation techniques. (These included placing bamboo shoots under the fingernails of captured soldiers to make them reveal secret information.) Therefore, the confrontations in the Pacific and Asian jungles between Japanese and Allied troops were as much clashes of culture as they were military battles. And as the Allies steadily pushed Japan's forces backward toward the home islands, increasing numbers of Japanese equated defeat with the destruction of their culture.

CARNAGE ON SAIPAN

The rash of wartime Japanese suicides reached a dramatic and grisly climax when U.S. troops attacked the tiny island of Saipan, in the Mariana Islands group, in June 1944. As the Americans fought their way across the island, the Japanese countered with numerous charges, hurling themselves in waves at U.S. machine guns and screaming "Banzai!" The largest such charge of the war occurred on Saipan on the night of July 6. More than three thousand Japanese, some with guns and bayonets, but many with no weapons at all, ran headlong at the amazed American troops. Many Americans died in the wild assault before all the attackers were killed. Several Japanese officers, including the famous Admiral Nagumo, then committed hara-kiri in nearby caves.

A few days later, these horrors were surpassed when hundreds of Japanese civilians gathered at the island's northern cliffs. They were terrified by propaganda stories about Americans brutalizing, raping, and killing prisoners. Rather than be captured, many parents threw their babies onto the rocks below, then jumped to their deaths. Others cut each other's throats, drowned themselves, or blew themselves up with hand grenades. Unable to stop them, American soldiers could only watch in utter horror and bewilderment.

SUPERIOR MILITARY MIGHT

The Americans and other Allies were able to keep the Japanese constantly on the defensive because of the vast superiority of American military might. Beginning late in 1942, the United States assembled the greatest concentration of naval strength in world history in the Pacific. By 1944 that military force was three times larger than Britain's and at least five times larger than Japan's. Most significantly, the number of American aircraft carriers had increased from three to more than a hundred by late 1944. Moreover, Admiral Nimitz made sure that each of his large warships was accompanied by a repair ship so that damaged vessels did not have to travel to distant bases for restoration.

These ships were increasingly loaded with new kinds of fighter aircraft, especially the F6F Hellcat. Designed to deal with the Japanese Zero fighter, "the Hellcat could outclimb and outdive its Japanese counterpart," says Ronald Spector. "It was 30 miles per hour faster, more heavily armed, and much better protected. By early 1944, one type of Hellcat—the F6FSN—was also being equipped with a new lightweight airborne radar."[48]

The United States also invented several new kinds of landing craft for assaults on the small Pacific islands. After ships and carrier planes bombarded a Japanese-held island, the landers swept ashore and discharged tanks, assault troops, guns, and supplies. One type of lander, the LST (landing ship tank), could carry up to twenty tanks and deliver them directly onto beaches. After completing this task, it was often used as a repair ship, a floating barracks to house troops, or a vessel to evacuate casualties. An LSM (landing ship medium) was similar to an LST, only smaller and more maneuverable; the LCI (landing craft infantry) carried between 200 and 250 infantrymen onto a beach; and the LCVP (landing craft, vehicle and

America's superior military arsenal included the LST (left), and the F6F Hellcat fighter plane.

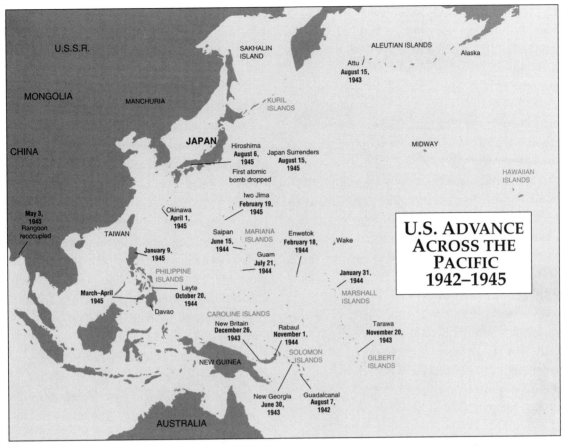

U.S. ADVANCE
ACROSS THE
PACIFIC
1942–1945

U.S.S.R.

SAKHALIN
ISLAND

ALEUTIAN ISLANDS

Alaska

Attu
August 15,
1943

MONGOLIA

MANCHURIA

KURIL
ISLANDS

CHINA

JAPAN

Hiroshima
August 6,
1945

First atomic
bomb dropped

Japan Surrenders
August 15,
1945

MIDWAY

HAWAIIAN
ISLANDS

May 3,
1945
Rangoon
reoccupied

TAIWAN

Okinawa
April 1,
1945

Iwo Jima
February 19,
1945

Saipan
June 15,
1944

MARIANA
ISLANDS

Enwetok
February 18,
1944

Wake

January 9,
1945

Guam
July 21,
1944

January 31,
1944

PHILIPPINE
ISLANDS

Leyte
October 20,
1944

MARSHALL
ISLANDS

March–April
1945

Davao

CAROLINE ISLANDS

New Britain
December 26,
1943

Rabaul
November 1,
1944

Tarawa
November 20,
1943

SOLOMON
ISLANDS

GILBERT
ISLANDS

NEW GUINEA

New Georgia
June 30,
1943

Guadalcanal
August 7,
1942

AUSTRALIA

personnel), the most common landing craft employed in the Pacific, carried thirty-six soldiers and one or two Jeeps or trucks.

As soon as the forces on these vehicles took control of a section of an island, more landers brought in special engineers called Seabees. Most of the islands taken had few roads or airfields, and many of the existing structures had been damaged in battle. So the Seabees quickly built roads, docks, bridges, and airfields. Once an island had been taken from the Japanese, it became a new American supply base, a stepping-stone in the unrelenting Allied march toward the Japanese homeland.

ONE HARD-WON VICTORY AFTER ANOTHER

During that march the Allies pounded Japanese strongholds into submission, racking up one hard-won victory after another. After taking Guadalcanal in early 1943, the Americans assaulted the nearby Russell Islands and then the Solomon chain, all north of Australia. Meanwhile, the Australians, aided by American forces under General MacArthur, secured the large island of New Guinea. The Japanese attempted to reinforce these areas, sending a convoy of twenty-two ships and twenty thousand men. On March 1, 1943,

U.S. planes spotted the convoy north of New Guinea and in the next few days demolished it. The Americans also retook the Gilbert, Marshall, and Caroline island chains, in the mid-Pacific, by February 1944.

Reaching the Mariana Islands, less than twelve hundred miles south of Japan, in mid-1944, the Americans met especially heavy resistance. On June 19 the Japanese tried to halt the American advance by attacking with a huge fleet of carriers and destroyers. In what later became known as the Battle of the Philippine Sea, or the "Great Mariana Turkey Shoot," U.S. planes shot down 330 of Japan's best planes and pilots and sank three Japanese carriers. Total U.S. losses amounted to only twenty-three planes. "One great advantage the American commanders had," San Jose State University scholar Harry A. Gailey points out,

> was their advanced air search radar capability—and an efficient organization to exploit it. Each carrier had a fighter director on board, and Lt. Joseph Eggert on the *Lexington* acted as the task force fighter director. These directors controlled not only the direction of intercept but also the number of fighters necessary for optimum use. A Japanese language specialist monitored the Japanese air coordinator's frequency, as the latter circled and gave directions to his pilots. Within seconds, the fighter directors had detailed information on enemy strength, altitude, and intentions.[49]

This greatest of all carrier battles of World War II proved a crushing defeat for Japan, one from which it simply could not recover.

But the struggle for the Marianas was far from over. The Japanese units on these islands refused to give up, and American land forces had to assault each island, in each case facing stubborn enemy resistance. The most appalling carnage occurred on Saipan. Rather than surrender, the defenders staged mass-suicide charges in which soldiers, often carrying only swords or even hobbling on crutches, threw themselves headlong into U.S machine guns and artillery, forcing the Americans to kill them. The Japanese commander sent a final message to Tokyo, saying, "We deeply apologize to the Emperor that we cannot do better."[50] Then he ordered his surviving men to charge the enemy and took his own life. Soon afterward, thousands of Japanese civilians on the island followed suit in a horrifying display of mass suicide. The total death toll of Japanese and Americans during the taking of this single tiny island exceeded fifty thousand.

THE RETAKING OF THE PHILIPPINES

One of the most important U.S. goals was to drive Japanese forces from the Philippines, which was Japan's vital supply and communications link with Southeast Asia. The American strategy of leapfrogging from island to island across the Pacific had proved highly effective. Now U.S. forces were poised to launch a major strike on Leyte Island in the central Philippines.

In mid-October 1944, a massive armada of six hundred warships and 250,000 men approached the target. First, American planes attacked Japanese airfields up and down the Philippine coasts, destroying more than three thousand enemy planes. On October 21, after bombers had weak- ened Japanese positions on Leyte, U.S. landing forces stormed ashore.

Only hours after the assault began, one landing craft came close to shore and discharged a tall man with a corncob pipe, none other than Douglas MacArthur, fulfilling his promise to return and liberate the Philippines. He and his staff, accompanied by General Carlos Romulo, the Filipino leader, waded proudly through the knee-deep water and onto the beach. In

PREPARING FOR DEATH

Following the ancient military code of the samurai, which taught that surrender was the ultimate disgrace, the kamikaze pilots sacrificed their lives in daring suicide attacks against U.S. ships. The name "kamikaze" came from the Japanese legend of the Divine Wind, which the sun goddess sent to destroy the Mongol invaders in the thirteenth century.

Most of the kamikaze pilots were young, in their teens or early twenties, with barely the amount of training needed to fly their death missions. Before taking off, they celebrated by drinking toasts to the emperor, the empire, and the glory of death and the afterlife. Many sang the "Kamikaze Song of the Warrior," which included the lines, "In serving on the seas, be a corpse saturated with water. . . . In serving in the sky, be a corpse that challenges the clouds. Let us all die close by the side of our royal leader."

Next, the pilots wrote their last letters to loved ones. "May our deaths," said one young man, "be as sudden and clean as the shattering of crystal." Another wrote, "We shall plunge into the enemy ships cherishing the conviction that Japan has been . . . a place where only lovely homes, brave women, and beautiful friendships are allowed to exist." And another pilot begged, "Most important of all, do not weep for me." Finishing their letters, they marched with heads held high to their planes and flew away to certain death.

General Douglas MacArthur (center) and his staff wade ashore on Leyte Island in the Philippines, fulfilling his vow to return and take the islands.

his first official statement, MacArthur announced:

> People of the Philippines! I have returned. By the Grace of Almighty God our forces stand again on Philippine soil—soil consecrated in the blood of our two peoples. . . . Rally to me. Let the indomitable [unbeatable] spirit of Bataan and Corregidor lead us on.[51]

As the American forces pushed inland on Leyte Island, the Japanese massed most of their remaining warships for a last desperate attempt to stop the invasion. Japanese strategists divided their force into three sections. The first would act as a decoy to lure the Americans away from the Leyte beachhead. Meanwhile, the other two sections of the fleet would sail around Leyte from the north and south and attack the U.S. fleet from the rear.

GUTS, GUMPTION, AND VICTORY AT SEA

Occurring over the course of nearly four days, from October 23 to 25, 1944, the Battle of Leyte Gulf was the greatest sea battle ever fought. It began with the utter destruction of the southernmost Japanese fleet by an American force commanded by Rear Admiral Jesse B. Oldendorf. As the Japanese ships emerged from the Surigao Strait, south of Leyte, their radar failed to detect the huge armada of U.S. destroyers and other warships that was poised like a cat waiting for a mouse to exit its lair. Oldendorf later wrote:

> Upon giving the orders to "open fire" it seemed as if every ship in the [American] flank forces and the battle line opened up at once, and there was a semi-circle of fire which landed squarely on one point, which was the leading [Japanese] battleship. The

semi-circle of fire so confused the Japanese that they did not know what target to shoot at.[52]

In the carnage and confusion, the Japanese ships kept emerging, more or less blindly, from the strait; and as they did so, the American forces continued to sink them one by one. Only one Japanese vessel survived. Oldendorf later said rather bluntly, "Never give a sucker a chance. If my opponent is foolish enough to come at me with an inferior force, I'm certainly not going to give him an even break."[53]

Meanwhile, the Japanese decoy ships succeeded in their mission of drawing a large portion of the American fleet away. And that left a tiny group of U.S. ships under the command of Rear Admiral Clifton A. Sprague to deal with the second and very large northern Japanese task force. Sprague reasoned that his own forces would likely be wiped out in less

The carrier USS Gambier Bay *comes under fire at the Battle of Leyte Gulf. Although the United States sustained heavy losses at Leyte Gulf, the Americans nearly destroyed the Japanese navy.*

than an hour; but he felt he had to try to delay the Japanese as long as possible. "If we can get this task force to attack us," he said, "we can delay its descent on Leyte until help comes, though obviously the end will come sooner for us."[54]

Sprague himself later compared the savage naval fight that followed to "a puppy being smacked by a truck."[55] Yet in this case, it was the truck, and not the puppy, that ended up being crushed. To the surprise and dismay of the Japanese, the greatly outnumbered and outgunned American forces staged one heroic and devastating attack after another. Small, quick, and maneuverable American torpedo boats weaved in and out among the larger enemy ships, using deadly hit-and-run tactics, all the while valiantly keeping the Japanese away from the beaches. Although Sprague's small forces sustained heavy casualties and damage, they managed to fight until the enemy withdrew in utter confusion. "I could not believe my eyes," Sprague later remarked of the Japanese retreat. "It took a whole series of reports from circling planes to convince me. And I still could not get the fact to soak into my battle-numbed brain. At best, I had expected to be swimming by this time."[56] Samuel Morison later commented:

> Because the enemy commander lacked gumption [raw courage], and Sprague had plenty; and also because the Japanese had no air support, a fleet more than ten times as powerful as the Americans in gunfire was defeated.[57]

Morison added, "In no engagement in its entire history has the United States Navy shown more gallantry, guts, and gumption."[58]

Heroics aside, in truth the horrific fighting in Leyte Gulf took its toll on both sides. The Americans lost one carrier, five other ships, and three thousand men. But the Japanese suffered a major and crippling defeat, losing four carriers, three battleships, nineteen destroyers, and some ten thousand men. Simply stated, the United States had effectively knocked the main surviving elements of the Japanese navy out of the war.

Still, the fighting in the Philippines dragged on for many months. On island after island, Japanese soldiers, with no hope of victory, forced the Americans to pay in blood for every square foot of territory. In July 1945 the battle for the Philippines finally ended. Japan had lost more than 400,000 of its best-trained fighting men. As for the Americans, they were back to stay. When MacArthur set foot on Corregidor, he ordered, "Hoist the colors and let no enemy ever haul them down."[59]

TIGHTENING THE NOOSE AROUND JAPAN

With the Marianas and Philippines retaken and the Japanese navy almost completely destroyed, Japan itself lay wide open to invasion by the Americans. The final assault called for a two-pronged offensive. First, U.S. forces would destroy Japanese merchant ships and cut supply

American bombers pound a Japanese cruiser. With the Philippines secure, the Americans could concentrate on attacking the islands of Japan.

lines by blockading Japan. The island nation would then be isolated from its outside sources of oil, coal, iron, foodstuffs, and other essential commodities. In the first months of 1945, the United States reduced Japan's flow of incoming supplies to a trickle, and many people in Japan began to hoard coal, food, and other goods.

The second aspect of the U.S. offensive was the repeated and massive bombing of Japanese cities, military installations, and industrial facilities. During these fateful months, the Americans dropped hundreds of thousands of tons of bombs on Japan. Many cities were leveled, including Tokyo, which burned almost to the ground on the night of March 9, 1945. U.S. Air Force commander Major General George C. Kenney warned, "Japan must surrender or the United States will strike Japan with 5,000 planes a day and reduce the country to a nation of nomads."[60]

An aerial photograph of Tokyo after massive bombing by U.S. planes shows the extent of the destruction. Many other Japanese cities were similarly leveled by U.S. bombing.

The combined blockade and bombing effort created unprecedented chaos in Japan. Most schools and other public institutions closed as millions of citizens fled from cities and towns into the countryside. With supplies dwindling and the country practically bankrupt, the Japanese people began to suffer as never before. Many now asked if continued fighting was worth the price. But the Japanese militarists refused even to think about surrender. "One hundred million die together" became their new catchphrase as they ruthlessly committed the nation to fight to the death. Japan was on the verge of complete collapse; yet tragically, its leaders could think of little else but saving face; so the devastation of their country continued.

JAPAN'S LAST-DITCH DEFENSIVE

In early 1945 the last two strategically important islands still held by the Japanese were Iwo Jima and Okinawa. Each was located only a few hundred miles south of Japan, and the Japanese considered them gateways to their homeland. So they transformed both islands into seemingly impenetrable fortresses by installing huge concrete walls, fields of land mines, and networks of underground tunnels. On Iwo Jima, for example, a patch of land only eight square miles in extent, a force of twenty-one thousand men carved eleven miles of tunnels and devised thousands of lethal booby traps. Enhancing the defenses, 550-foot Mount Suribachi, on the southern end of the island, was honeycombed with caves and holes perfect for snipers.

To soften up the island for the landing forces, American planes pounded Iwo Jima with explosives for seventy-five days, dropping more than forty thousand bombs in the last three days alone. Then, on February 19, some thirty thousand U.S. Marines stormed ashore. The fighting soon proved to be the bloodiest of an already bloody war—chaotic, merciless, and horribly destructive for all concerned. The Japanese defenders fought relentlessly after their commander gave them the following order:

We shall infiltrate into the midst of the enemy and annihilate them. We shall grasp bombs, charge the enemy tanks and destroy them. With every salvo we will, without fail, kill the enemy. Each man will make it his duty to kill ten of the enemy before dying![61]

Many Americans experienced this suicidal brand of determination as they struggled furiously for possession of every square inch of the tiny island. One U.S. Marine found a seriously wounded Japanese soldier trying to get his heavy machine gun into action. The American literally emptied his ammo clip into the other man, yet the Japanese soldier refused to go

SINKING THE *YAMATO*

On April 6, 1945, in an attempt to meet the American attack on Okinawa, what remained of the Japanese fleet sailed from Japan. One of these vessels was the 70,000-ton *Yamato,* the largest battleship ever built. Accompanying it was the cruiser *Yahagi* and an escort of eight destroyers. The next day 386 U.S. planes found the Japanese ships and moved in for a deadly assault. Since all available Japanese planes were now being used by the kamikazes, the *Yamato* and its small escort vessels had no air cover, so the ships were sitting ducks. The American planes attacked in three waves, scoring nearly twenty direct hits on the *Yamato.* Helldiver attack craft from the USS *Bennington* scored hits near *Yamato*'s large smokestack at 12:41 P.M. At 12:45 an American Avenger attack plane torpedoed the battleship's bow, opening a wide gash near the waterline. The Japanese fired back with every machine gun and antiaircraft weapon aboard. But these defensive measures could not stop the savage American attack. The *Yamato* finally exploded in a gigantic fireball and sank, taking with it Japan's dreams of world conquest.

U.S. Marines raise the American flag over Mount Suribachi on Iwo Jima.
The fighting on Iwo Jima was the bloodiest of the war.

down; finally out of ammunition, the marine had to stab repeatedly with his knife to dispatch his opponent.

Meanwhile, the Japanese snipers hiding underground took a heavy toll. Typically, they waited until one or more American soldiers were only a few feet away and then opened fire. The Americans countered with deadly handheld and tank-mounted flamethrowers, which poured out streams of burning liquid, incinerating the enemy. For days savage

hand-to-hand combat raged, the opponents using knives, bayonets, and even their bare hands when their bullets ran out. The attackers took a full three days to capture a mere seven hundred yards of territory.

During the morning of February 23, a marine patrol fought its way to the summit of Mount Suribachi and raised the U.S. flag. Associated Press photographer Joe Rosenthal was with them; and he snapped the now world-famous photo immortalizing that triumphant moment. But it took the Americans nearly another month to secure the entire island. The final death toll was grim: 6,821 Americans killed, almost 18,000 wounded, and nearly 21,000 Japanese killed. Moreover, the scars of battle lingered. Maria Tallen, a USO performer who entertained troops in the months following the battle, recalled that arms, heads, and other body parts continued to wash in with the tide. "There were rows of white crosses as far as the eye could see," she later said, "and I wept at the overwhelming horror of it all."[62] In all, the Japanese lost more than 130,000 men defending Iwo Jima and Okinawa. And though ultimately victorious, the Americans lost more than 19,000.

As the Americans continued to close in on Japan, the country's military leaders next chose mass-suicide attacks as a last line of defense. Japanese officers created special units of suicide pilots known as kamikazes, Japanese for "divine wind." These men adhered to the motto "in death there is life," believing that they would be honored in the afterlife for bravely dying for their country. Thousands of them purposely crashed their aircraft, which were filled with explosives, into American ships; trying to insult the enemy, some screamed, "Babe Ruth, go to hell!" as they dived at their targets. Desperate U.S. gunners shot down many of the suicide planes, but many more fulfilled their mission. In all, the kamikazes sank thirty-four ships and damaged 288, including the mighty carrier *Enterprise*.

DEMANDS FOR JAPAN'S SURRENDER

The naked truth, however, was that even the bloody sacrifices of Japan's young pilots were not enough to help the collapsing Japanese empire. Unable to match the incredible might of the United States and other Allied nations, Japan's fate was quite literally sealed. On several occasions in early 1945, President Roosevelt called upon the Japanese to surrender. But all of these demands were summarily refused.

Then, on April 12, 1945, at the height of the fighting in Okinawa, the world was shocked by the news that Roosevelt had died suddenly of a stroke. Winston Churchill lamented that it was a bitter loss to humanity. And similar sentiments came from people across the United States. One New Yorker observed that it was regrettable that the nation's leader did not live long enough to enjoy the victory and peace he had worked so hard to create. Many felt that the spirit of the American war effort had died with Roosevelt. But another New Yorker offered the comforting thought, "Don't worry. . . . His plans are made and somebody's gonna carry them out."[63]

That "somebody" was Roosevelt's vice president, Harry S Truman, who was sworn in as the nation's thirty-third president only hours after Roosevelt's death. The job of finishing off Japan now belonged to Truman, who told the press, "I don't know if any of you fellows ever had a load of hay or bull fall on him, but last night the whole weight of the moon and stars fell on me. I feel a tremendous responsibility. Please pray for me."[64]

Truman, like Roosevelt, called for the Japanese to surrender unconditionally, that is, without receiving any special terms or deals. But the Japanese militarists refused and continued their defiant stance. Even though their military forces were crippled and their economy devastated, they still refused to give up, believing that the Japanese people could withstand whatever the United States and Allies could throw at them. They did not know, as Truman did, that throughout the war, American scientists had been developing a secret, unbelievably powerful weapon, one that had the strength to bring any nation to its knees. And in the summer of 1945, it would be ready for use.

Chapter 6
Nuclear Dawn: The United States Drops the Atomic Bomb

After the United States captured the Japanese stronghold of Okinawa in late June 1945, the Americans and other Allies began preparations for the greatest undertaking of a war already characterized by monumental undertakings. Two sweeping military plans—Operation Olympic and Operation Coronet, collectively part of Operation Downfall—would begin the massive invasion of the Japanese home islands. The first major target, Kyūshū, the southernmost large island in the group, would be assaulted in Operation Olympic in November 1945; then Operation Coronet, the invasion of the main island of Honshū, would begin in March 1946.

American planners fully expected that these assaults would be time-consuming and extremely bloody; clearly, the Japanese would stage a massive and desperate resistance and probably resort to suicidal attacks that would kill and injure many of the invaders. Douglas MacArthur predicted that before it was over Operation Downfall would "cost over a million casualties to American forces alone."[65] By "casualties," he meant both dead and wounded. A number of his colleagues

agreed that American casualties would be huge. Admiral William D. Leahy, for example, told President Truman that American troops had suffered about 35 percent casualties in taking Okinawa. Assuming that the attack on Kyūshū would produce similar results, Leahy estimated that 268,000 Americans would be killed or wounded in taking that single island (based on the total of 767,000 soldiers scheduled to take part). Military experts warned the president that, in addition, dozens of American ships would likely be struck and sunk by kamikaze planes.

Truman and other Allied leaders were appalled by these grim estimates; and in retrospect, they were greatly relieved that this climactic and horrendously costly invasion of Japan never occurred. Instead, the war came to an abrupt and decisive end in a way no one could have predicted as little as a year before. As soldiers died by the thousands on the beaches of Iwo Jima and Okinawa, American scientists secretly labored to put the finishing touches on the most terrifying weapon ever devised. Only a handful of American and Allied leaders knew that the scientists had been working on the device since 1939.

Harry S Truman

Raised on a Missouri farm, Harry Truman (1884–1972) earned the nick-name "Give 'em hell Harry" for his courage and frankness. He served with distinction on the fields of France in World War I, fighting in several major battles. After returning home in 1919, he married Elizabeth (Bess) Wallace, his childhood sweetheart. Truman then operated a clothing store in Kansas City. After the store went out of business, he entered public service, working his way up through a number of local political offices. In 1934 he became a U.S. senator, and in 1944 he was President Roosevelt's running mate.

On April 12, 1945, Roosevelt died and Truman became president. The huge responsibilities of running the mammoth war effort and leading the free world now rested on Truman's shoulders. He worked hard to carry out Roosevelt's plans for the defeat of the Axis powers. The most important decision of Truman's life came only months later, when he

chose to drop atomic bombs on two Japanese cities. After the war Truman played an important role in the creation of the United Nations and won the presidential election of 1948. Most historians remember him as one of the hardest-working, most honest, and most intelligent of the country's presidents.

The decision to drop atomic bombs on Japan was the toughest and most important decision of President Harry Truman's life.

BIRTH OF THE MANHATTAN PROJECT

The effort to develop an atomic bomb was code-named the Manhattan Project. It was the culmination of a series of important scientific discoveries made in the 1920s and 1930s. Noted researchers such as Albert Einstein, Danish physicist Niels Bohr, and British physicist Ernest Rutherford studied the structure and behavior of atoms, the tiny building blocks that make up all matter. Among other things, they recognized that splitting atoms of uranium and other radioactive elements released unusually large amounts of energy.

To escape Europe's Axis dictatorships, many of the world's leading atomic scientists, including Einstein, Bohr, and Italy's Enrico Fermi, moved to the United States in the late 1930s. There, they continued with their research into the splitting of the atom, a process called fission. It did not take these scientists long to realize that the energy released during fission might be utilized in a weapon of enormous destructive power. The race to develop such a weapon began with a historic letter from Einstein to President Roosevelt on August 2, 1939. Einstein asserted:

> It may become possible to set up a nuclear chain reaction in a large mass of uranium, by which vast amounts of power . . . would be generated. . . . Now it appears almost certain that this could be achieved in the immediate future. This new phenomenon would also lead to the construction of bombs, and it is conceivable . . . that extremely powerful bombs of a new type may thus be constructed. A single bomb of this type, carried by boat and exploded in a port, might very well destroy the whole port, together with some of the surrounding territory. . . . In view of this situation, you may think it desirable to have some permanent contact maintained between the administration and the group of physicists working on chain reactions in America.[66]

Accepting Einstein's suggestion, Roosevelt and Winston Churchill almost immediately launched the huge and highly secret Manhattan Project. They felt there was good reason for haste. Allied spies reported that German scientists might also be developing atomic bombs, which Hitler would surely use against Britain and eventually against the United States. This fear kept scientists working on the Manhattan Project at an ever-increasing pace. In addition, most of the few U.S. leaders who knew about the effort believed that such a bomb was just what the country needed to win the war in a quick and decisive fashion.

THE ROAR THAT WARNED OF DOOMSDAY

The Manhattan Project was the most complex and costly scientific endeavor in history. It ended up costing the United States and Britain $2.5 billion, a tremendous sum at the time. The project involved scientists, military personnel, and labs all over the United States. Henry L. Stimson, the U.S. secretary of war, headed the president's committee that decided how the bomb would be developed and delivered. Dr. J. Robert Oppenheimer led the scientific team, and Major General Leslie R. Groves commanded the Army Corps of Engineers, whose task was to build the device. The government built two huge plants for bomb construction. One was in Oak Ridge, Tennessee, the other in Richland, Washington. Oppenheimer and his team of scientists worked at a special lab at Los Alamos, in the desert near Santa Fe, New Mexico.

Security was extremely tight. Although more than 200,000 people helped produce the bomb, only a tiny handful knew what they were actually working on. Even Vice President Truman knew nothing of the project until he was sworn in to succeed Roosevelt in April 1945. In short, those in charge made sure that it was the "best-kept secret of the war."

The atomic age began on July 16, 1945, when Oppenheimer's and Groves's units conducted a test firing of the new super-weapon in the desert near Alamogordo, New Mexico. Although most of those working on the project believed the device would work, no one was prepared for the awesome power the weapon actually possessed. The large steel tower that

FISSION CREATES ATOMIC ENERGY

Fission occurs when a microscopic particle traveling at high speed strikes the nucleus (center) of a large radioactive atom such as uranium 235. The nucleus splits and sends out more of these particles. These then hit other nearby atoms, splitting them apart, and the process quickly speeds up. Each time an atom splits, a small amount of energy is released as a by-product. As more and more atoms split, a chain reaction takes place and a huge amount of energy is generated in the form of heat and light. An atomic bomb works by forcing a mass of radioactive material to undergo an uncontrolled chain reaction. The potential energy locked within atoms is so great that a mass of fissionable material weighing only a few pounds can destroy a city.

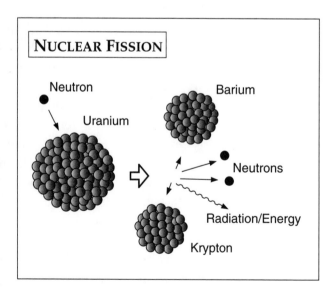

Workers construct the tower that will hold the first atomic bomb at the Atomic Test site at Almogordo, New Mexico. The blast vaporized the tower.

held the bomb was completely vaporized in the first second of the explosion. Windows rattled 250 miles away, and a blinding light momentarily banished the early morning darkness. General Thomas R. Farrell, who witnessed the test from a bunker five miles away, later described the spectacle:

> The effects could well be called . . . magnificent, beautiful, stupendous, and terrifying. . . . The lighting effects beggared description. The whole country was lighted . . . with an intensity many times that of the midday sun. It was golden, purple, violet, gray, and blue. . . . Thirty seconds after the explosion, came, first the air blast, pressing hard against people and things . . . followed almost immediately by the strong, sustained, awesome roar which warned of doomsday and made us feel that we puny things were blasphemous to dare tamper with the forces heretofore [formally] reserved to the Almighty.[67]

Major General Leslie R. Groves (left) commanded the Army Corps of Engineers whose task it was to build the atomic bomb. Dr. J. Robert Oppenheimer (right) led the team of scientists who designed the bomb.

Shortly after the test, Secretary Stimson and President Truman, who were meeting overseas with Churchill and the Soviet leader, Joseph Stalin, received news of its success. The first message from Washington, D.C., read: "Operated on this morning, diagnosis not yet complete, but results seem satisfactory and already exceed expectations."[68] The message was worded to look like an innocent personal medical matter, in case it fell into the wrong hands. A few hours later a second message came, advising Stimson:

Doctor has just returned most enthusiastic and confident that the little boy is as husky as his big brother. The light in his eyes discernible from here to Highhold [Stimson's home on Long Island, New York] and I could have heard his screams from here to my farm.[69]

The "little boy" and his "big brother" were not Stimson's sons, of course, but the bomb that had just been detonated in New Mexico and another that was being prepared for delivery on a Japanese city.

THE DECISION TO DROP THE BOMB

Truman and his advisers considered several factors in deciding whether or not to use the new atomic device. A few of the president's advisers argued that using the bomb would be morally wrong. They pointed out that the weapon's blast would be so huge that there would be no way to avoid killing thousands of civilians while striking at military targets. They were also against using the bomb because it was not needed, they claimed. The ongoing blockade and bombing of Japanese cities had already nearly destroyed Japan. According to this view, it was only a matter of time before the enemy would have to surrender. One of those expressing this view was General Dwight D. Eisenhower, commander of the Allied forces in Europe and a future U.S. president. He told Stimson privately that using the bomb was "completely unnecessary."[70] Furthermore, Eisenhower suggested, dropping such a destructive weapon might cause the civilized nations of the world to condemn the United States.

But President Truman and Secretary Stimson were unmoved by these arguments. They had weighed the consequences of *not* using the bomb. U.S. strategists told the president that the invasion of Japan would take a year or more and would cost at least half a million American and several million Japanese lives. And Stimson pointed out that the Japanese would likely fight to the death. It was better, he said, to kill a few thousand

HORROR AT SEA

After being damaged by a kamikaze attack on March 31, 1945, the USS *Indianapolis* docked in San Francisco for repairs. There, it received its orders to deliver the uranium for the first atomic bomb, or A-bomb, to Tinian Island, in the Marianas. On July 30, only four days after completing its mission to Tinian, the *Indianapolis* suffered a fatal hit from a torpedo launched by a Japanese submarine. The ship sank so fast, there was no time to send out a call for help. For more than two days, no one knew it had gone down, so no relief vessels were sent. Of the twelve hundred men aboard the doomed ship, eight hundred survived the attack. They spent nearly three and a half days in the ocean, with no food, no drinking water, and no way to sleep or even rest. The ordeal was made worse when swarms of sharks attacked, dragging hundreds of sailors to gruesome deaths. Managing to beat the sharks back with boards and other debris, 316 of the *Indianapolis* crew survived long enough to be rescued.

with the bomb and end the war quickly than allow millions to die in an invasion. Also, he insisted, the United States should not be moved by moral considerations. After all, the Japanese had not been concerned about the morality of their sneak attack on Pearl Harbor, the savage mistreatment of American prisoners, and the brutal kamikaze attacks. Truman agreed and later wrote, "I regarded the bomb as a weapon and never had any doubt that it should be used."[71] In addition, Winston Churchill sent word that he favored the bomb's use if it could bring an early end to the war.

Having determined that they would drop the bomb, the American leaders now had to choose the targets. Some said that Kyōto, the ancient capital, should be destroyed first. But Stimson disagreed, pointing out that the city housed Japan's greatest cultural and religious shrines and therefore, to preserve the core elements of Japanese culture, it should be spared. Truman agreed, writing in his private journal, "Even if the Japs are savages, ruthless, merciless and fanatic, we as the leader of the free world for the common welfare cannot drop this terrible bomb on the old capital or the new [Tokyo]."[72] The initial targets finally agreed on were Hiroshima, Kikura, Niigata, and Nagasaki, all centers of industry and war production.

FLIGHT OF THE *ENOLA GAY*

The final series of events leading to the dropping of the atomic bomb went like clockwork. On July 24, 1945, the U.S. cruiser *Indianapolis* delivered lead buckets containing the uranium needed for the bomb to Tinian Island in the Marianas. The captain of the ship was unaware of the contents of the buckets. His orders were that if his ship sank, he should save the containers at all costs, putting them in lifeboats if necessary. That same day planes from the United States arrived with other essential bomb parts. Scientists on Tinian assembled the first bomb, nicknamed Little Boy, during the next few days, but they did not arm it, fearing that if the plane carrying it crashed during takeoff, the entire island would be vaporized. They decided instead to arm the weapon in the air shortly before reaching the target.

As a prelude to the atomic attack, on July 26, 1945, the United States and the Allies issued a final ultimatum to Japan. "We call upon the government of Japan," the message read, "to proclaim now the unconditional surrender of all Japan's armed forces and to provide proper and adequate assurances of their good faith in such action." With a subtle warning about the impending atomic destruction, the message concluded, "The alternative for Japan is prompt and utter destruction." When the Japanese refused to accept the ultimatum, Truman grimly commented that there was "no alternative now."[73]

On August 5, 1945, technicians on Tinian loaded the world's first nuclear weapon to be used in war onto a B-29 called the *Enola Gay*. The pilot, Colonel Paul Tibbets, had named the plane after his mother. Two other B-29s, carrying military observers and cameras, were to

The crew of the Enola Gay. Pilot Paul Tibbets stands in the center.

accompany the *Enola Gay*. The planes glided off the Tinian runway at 2:45 A.M. on August 6.

The planes reached the initial target, Hiroshima, a city of 340,000, at about 8:13 A.M. Major Thomas Ferebee, the *Enola Gay*'s bombardier, peered through his bombsight and recognized the city's various landmarks, which he had virtually memorized from studying photos taken by military aircraft weeks before. To incur maximum destruction, he had been trained to release the bomb so that it would fall directly over Aioi Bridge. This was an immensely difficult task; the plane was flying at an altitude of 31,600 feet and moving at a speed of 285 miles per hour, and the bomb itself would therefore begin its downward journey with the same forward momentum. At 8:15 Ferebee was confident he was ready and signaled the rest of the crew. All but Tibbets, who was at the aircraft's controls, pulled on the special dark glasses they had been issued

A mushroom cloud from the atomic bomb explosion rises over Hiroshima. The explosion was so massive and violent it razed the city and killed tens of thousands of people.

to prevent the brilliant light of the blast from blinding them. Then Ferebee took a deep breath and discharged the more than four-ton Little Boy. Suddenly, the plane, instantly some nine thousand pounds lighter, lurched upward, after which Tibbets banked the aircraft away at a steep angle in order to avoid the effects of the coming blast. Only then did he pull on his own dark goggles.

A few seconds later, the bomb automatically detonated at an altitude of eighteen hundred feet. An arc of blinding light seemed to tear the sky apart. "My God!" murmured a startled crew member. Another later recalled, "Suddenly a glaring whitish pink light appeared in the sky accompanied by an unnatural tremor that was followed almost immediately by a wave of suffocating heat and wind that swept everything away in its path."[74] As a gigantic mushroom cloud rose into the atmosphere, Tibbets swung the plane around for a better view. "My God, what have we done?" one stunned crewman asked. Another exclaimed, "Good God, could anyone live through that down there?"[75] Tibbets himself later remembered, "The thing reminded me . . . of a boiling pot of tar. . . . It was black and boiling underneath with a steam haze on top of it."[76] Tibbets added that he could not see the city at all through the layer of dust.

IN A NIGHTMARISH LANDSCAPE

In fact, there was little left to see, for most of Hiroshima had simply ceased to exist. Four of the city's six square miles, including fully 80 percent of all buildings, had been flattened. The searing heat had melted steel girders like candle wax, and people who had been standing near the center of the blast had been totally vaporized, leaving only their shadows burned into nearby concrete walls. Tens of thousands of people lay dead; tens of thousands more had been seriously injured by heat, flying clouds of glass, wood, and other debris; and most of the pitiful survivors were trapped in a nightmarish landscape of radioactive rubble.

Some of those who had survived in one piece combed through the ruins attempting to rescue the legions of wounded and dying. Among these heroic but largely futile efforts was that of a priest, Father Kleinsorge, who, according to a later chronicler,

got lost on a detour around a fallen tree, and as he looked for his way . . . he heard a voice ask. . . "Have you anything to drink?" He saw a uniform. Thinking there was just one soldier, he approached with water. [Then] he saw there were about twenty men, and they were all in exactly the same nightmarish state. Their faces were wholly burned, their eyesockets hollow, the fluid from their melted eyes had run down their cheeks. . . . Their mouths were mere swollen, pus-covered wounds, which they could not bear to stretch enough to admit the [water].[77]

Meanwhile, huge, very strange drops of rain began to fall on the ruins. "The rising cloud column had carried moisture sufficiently high for water vapor to condense," John Toland writes,

and stained by radioactive dust, [to] fall in large drops. The "black rain," weird and almost supernatural, horrified the survivors. . . . It pelted down on the half-naked people, leaving gray streaks on their bodies, releasing in many of them a sense of awareness of the unimaginable disaster that had been visited on Hiroshima.[78]

Incredibly, even in the midst of this unparalleled devastation and horror, national beliefs and traditions remained uppermost in the minds of many. Four men staggered through the streets carrying a large portrait of the emperor, which they had risked their lives to rescue from a burning building. And everywhere they went, wounded people clawed their way to their feet to salute or bow to the picture as it went by.

"A RAIN OF RUIN"

World reactions to the bombing of Hiroshima were immediate and emotional. Not surprisingly, the shocked Japanese war leaders called the destruction "barbaric." Radio Tokyo reported:

The impact of the bomb is so terrific that practically all living things, human and animals, literally were seared to death by the tremendous heat and pressure engendered by the blast. All the dead and injured were burned beyond recognition.[79]

Early estimates suggested that more than seventy thousand people had died in the initial blast alone. And more were per-

The destruction of Hiroshima was complete and devastating. Yet Japan's leaders still refused to surrender.

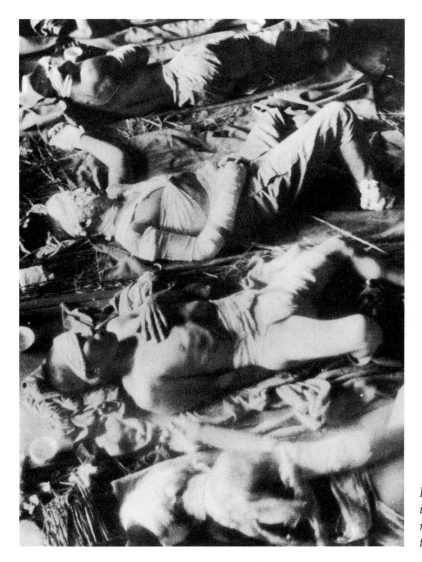

Hiroshima residents burned in the bomb blast. Fires raged in the city long after the initial attack.

ishing each hour from serious injuries or in the fires that raged through the ruins. The Japanese leaders charged, "This diabolical weapon brands the United States for ages to come as a destroyer of justice and mankind."[80]

President Truman announced the official U.S. position on August 7, saying, "The force from which the sun draws its power has been loosed upon those who brought war to the Far East." The president warned, "If they [the Japanese] do not now accept our terms, they may expect a rain of ruin from the air, the like of which has never been seen on this earth."[81]

Still, the Japanese leaders refused to surrender. So the Americans flew over large areas of Japan and dropped leaflets, which read in Japanese:

America asks that you take immediate heed of what we say in this leaflet. We are in possession of the most destructive explosive ever devised by man. . . . We have just begun to use this weapon against your homeland. If you have any doubt, make inquiry as to what happened to Hiroshima. . . . We ask that you now petition the Emperor to end the war. . . . You should take steps now to cease military resistance. Otherwise, we shall resolutely employ this bomb and all our other superior weapons to promptly and forcefully end the war.[82]

When this tactic also failed to convince the Japanese to surrender, a group of B-29s dropped a second atomic bomb two days later, on August 9. This time, the target was Nagasaki, a city of 250,000 located on the island of Kyūshū. The nearly total destruction of the city sent a wave of fear through the country. Japanese leaders met that night to debate surrender. The most extreme militarists argued that the country should fight on and that every Japanese citizen should die rather than surrender. Those who felt that surrender was better than annihilation called on Emperor Hirohito to decide. For years the Japanese people had fought a bloody war for the honor of their "living god." Now, as they teetered on the brink of total destruction, their fate was truly in his hands.

Chapter

7 "That Peace Be Now Restored": Surrender and Aftermath

On the night of August 9, 1945, when the most powerful of Japan's leaders met to discuss the Allied surrender terms, no one in the room doubted that the outlook for the nation was grim. All over the empire, Japanese armies had been crushed and defeated. The Imperial Navy was gone. The United States had Japan surrounded and blockaded and had demolished more than one hundred cities with conventional bombs. Even worse, only hours before the meeting, the second of the new superbombs had obliterated Nagasaki. The United States now threatened to use more A-bombs and blast Japan back into the Stone Age.

THE DECISION TO SURRENDER

The Japanese leadership was more or less evenly divided between those who wanted to continue fighting and those who thought surrender was the only sane option. In a tumultuous meeting, General Yoshijiro Umezu, a hardened militarist, told War Minister Tōjō:

> With luck we will be able to repulse the invaders before they land. At any rate I can say with confidence that we

will be able to destroy the major part of an invading force. That is, we will be able to inflict extremely heavy damage on the enemy.[83]

But though he himself was a right-wing militarist, Tōjō could not see the logic of

Japanese war minister Hideki Tōjō proposed seeking a workable peace with the Americans.

this approach. Even if the army *could* inflict such casualties on the invaders, he asked Umezu, what good would it do? The Allies would only send a second wave, and then a third. Sooner or later, the Japanese forces would crumble. It would be better, said Tōjō, to seek some kind of workable peace with the Americans now and save further bloodshed.

Similar arguments raged back and forth for several more hours until the two sides agreed to ask the emperor to break the deadlock. In a separate meeting, Hirohito told them:

> I have given serious thought to the situation prevailing at home and abroad and have concluded that continuing the war means destruction for the nation and a prolongation of bloodshed and cruelty in the world. I cannot bear to see my innocent people suffer any longer. . . . It goes without saying that it is unbearable for me to see the brave and loyal fighting men of Japan disarmed. It is equally unbearable that others who have rendered me devoted service should now be punished as instigators of the war. Nevertheless, the time has come when we must bear the unbearable. . . . I swallow my own tears and give my sanction to the proposal to accept the Allied proclamation.[84]

Essentially, Hirohito and those who agreed with him expressed the desire that the surrender be accepted on one condition—that the status of the emperor be preserved. The "living god" must be allowed to continue as a figurehead for the Japanese people. The proposal was transmitted to the Allies the next day.

The Americans, too, were divided about surrender terms. Hearing the Japanese condition, a number of U.S. leaders angrily advised the president to reject the proposal. One congressman said, "Let the Japs know . . . what unconditional surrender means. Let the dirty rats squeal."[85] But others were more willing to compromise. Secretary Stimson, with his usual voice of reason, pointed out that the emperor was perhaps the only person who could order the Japanese armies all over Southeast Asia to surrender peacefully. Agreeing to the emperor's condition was the only way of saving "us from a score of bloody Iwo Jimas and Okinawas," Stimson said.[86]

Truman agreed with Stimson and the Americans compromised. They sent word to the Japanese that the surrender would have to remain unconditional. The status of the emperor would be decided by the supreme commander of the Allied forces and by a public ballot of the Japanese people. Essentially, this meant that if all went well, the emperor would be retained.

TO ENDURE THE UNENDURABLE

Perhaps predictably, the Japanese war hawks were upset by the Allied reply. And arguments among them dragged on for four more days. Finally, the emperor, who was clearly growing impatient, told the war leaders:

> I have listened carefully to all of the arguments opposing Japan's accep-

NEVER SURRENDER

Marooned on tiny remote Pacific islands, some Japanese soldiers did not know when the war ended. Rescuers found many of them in the months following the surrender. A few soldiers, however, either never found out or refused to believe that the conflict was over. In 1951 nineteen Japanese soldiers on one of the Mariana Islands finally surrendered. Meanwhile, Hiru Onada and Kinishi Kozuka held out on a small Philippine island for decades because their commander had ordered them never to surrender. After being discovered in 1972, they exchanged gunfire with Philippine police and Kozuka was killed. Onada then hid in the forest. In 1974 his former commander flew to the island and persuaded him to give up. Former private Teruo Nakamura discovered the war was over in 1975 after hiding out on an island in Indonesia for thirty-three years. During all that time, he believed in his heart that Japan had won the war and that his people would eventually come to take him home. Some Japanese authorities believe that a few other Japanese troops continue to maintain the honor of the empire in forgotten corners of the wide Pacific.

tance of the Allied reply as it stands, but my own view has not changed. . . . Some seem to question the Allied motives in regard to the supreme power of the Emperor, but I . . . do not believe the [Allied] note was written to subvert our [national traditions].

Hirohito's voice broke momentarily; it was clear to all that he was emotionally upset. "All these feelings are so hard to bear," he continued, "but I cannot let my subjects suffer any longer. . . . It is my desire that all of you, my ministers of state, bow to my wishes and accept the Allied reply forthwith."[87]

A few hours later, on August 15, 1945, Emperor Hirohito issued a radio broadcast to the Japanese people, almost none of whom had ever before heard his voice. He emphasized the terrible losses his country had already sustained and then mentioned the "most cruel bomb" the enemy had begun to employ. "Should we continue to fight," he said,

it would not only result in the ultimate collapse and obliteration of the Japanese nation, but also . . . the total extinction of human civilization. . . . The hardships and sufferings to which our nation is to be subjected hereafter will certainly be great. . . .

Japanese emperor Hirohito. In an August 15 radio broadcast he told the Japanese people he had decided to surrender to the Allies.

However, it is according to the dictate of time and fate that We have resolved to pave the way for a grand peace for all the generations to come by enduring the unendurable and suffering what is insufferable.[88]

The Japanese people reacted first with disbelief, then with grief and shame. But nearly all did their best to support the decision of their emperor.

THE GUNS SILENT AT LAST

In the two weeks following the emperor's fateful broadcast, a huge array of American and British warships converged on Japan. For some Japanese, the ancient fear and loathing of the foreign black ships was now translated into grim reality. Hundreds of landing craft and transport planes poured more than twenty thousand occupation troops into the home islands. Meanwhile, into Tokyo Bay cruised the 45,000-ton USS *Missouri,* flagship of the U.S. Pacific Fleet, followed by dozens of Allied support ships.

The formal surrender came on Sunday morning, September 2, 1945, three years, eight months, and twenty-five days after Japanese planes had attacked Pearl Harbor. A nine-member Japanese delegation, led by Foreign Minister Mamoru Shigemitsu, boarded the *Missouri,* where hundreds of U.S. and other Allied officers waited. The Japanese were tense, obviously gripped by emotion, yet highly dignified. They walked to the table on which rested the surrender documents.

Then Douglas MacArthur, representing the Allied forces, approached the microphone and said:

> We are gathered here, representatives of the major warring powers, to conclude a solemn agreement whereby peace may be restored. . . . It is my earnest hope and indeed the hope of all mankind that from this solemn occasion a better world shall emerge out of the blood and carnage of the past— a world founded upon faith and understanding—a world dedicated to the dignity of man and the fulfillment of his most cherished wish—for freedom, tolerance, and justice.[89]

General MacArthur signs the surrender documents on board the USS Missouri *on September 2, 1945.*

When MacArthur finished speaking, the Japanese sat at the table and signed the documents. Then MacArthur signed, along with other Allied leaders, including Admiral Nimitz and the representatives of China, Great Britain, Australia, the Soviet Union, Canada, France, the Netherlands, and New Zealand. Finally, General MacArthur spoke again: "Let us pray that peace be now restored to the world and that God will preserve it always. These proceedings are closed."[90] Seconds later a gigantic flight of some two thousand Allied planes passed over the ship, and then over Tokyo, in a final, majestic demonstration of power. In Louis Snyder's words, "Thus, came to an end the long, tragic trail from Bataan and Corregidor through New Guinea, the Marianas, and the Philippines to Japan. The guns at last were silent."[91]

Those guns had caused death and destruction on a vast scale. The staggering human losses of the Pacific War were more than 17 million killed. This included 13 million Chinese, 1.7 million Japanese soldiers and civilians, more than 50,000 Americans, 40,000 British, 30,000 Australians, and 10,000 New Zealanders, among others. The wounded among all nationalities exceeded 20 million; and at least 10 million children became orphans. The material and economic losses were equally huge, in dollar figures running into the tens of billions.

JAPAN RISES FROM THE ASHES

The lost lives, of course, could never be replaced; yet the physical devastation *could.*

Moreover, the Americans and other Allies recognized that they must repair more than just their own damages. To allow their former enemies to languish and suffer on the ash heaps of their ruined cities would have violated the civilized, democratic, and humanitarian beliefs the Allies held dear. Accordingly, with MacArthur acting as supreme Allied commander, the United States began the tremendous task of rebuilding Japan and making it an ally, rather than a foe, of the free world. This official Allied policy was carried out in Germany and Italy as well. In Japan Emperor Hirohito joined in the effort, instructing his people to win the confidence of the world by obeying Japan's commitments to the surrender terms.

One of the first orders of business was to eliminate the aggressive elements of Japanese society that might cause trouble in the future. MacArthur ordered the new Japanese leaders to remove more than 200,000 militaristic politicians, army officers, and local leaders from their posts. Twenty-five of Japan's top-ranking leaders were tried as war criminals for giving the orders in Japan's war of aggression. Seven, including the infamous Tōjō, received death sentences and died by hanging on December 23, 1948. The other eighteen went to prison. In addition, more than five thousand "minor" war criminals were convicted of crimes such as the murder and mistreatment of prisoners of war. About one thousand of these men received death sentences.

In 1947 MacArthur introduced a new constitution for Japan. It set up independent courts and judges, gave guarantees

"Carryover" Wars of the Pacific Conflict

In this excerpt from their fascinating book, Dirty Little Secrets of World War II, *scholars James F. Dunnigan and Albert A. Nofi argue that a number of smaller later wars were in a sense continuations of the Pacific War.*

"There were a lot of 'supplementary wars' that followed. . . . This lingering combat occurred because, as usually happens in a major war, there were also a lot of little wars going on at the same time. While the big nations were slugging it out, the simultaneous little wars tended to go unnoticed. But when the principal nations decided to declare the war over, many of the minor players fought on. . . . The Communists had their hand in many of the 'carryover' wars. The one most Americans will recognize is Vietnam. During World War II, the Allies supported armed Vietnamese resistance groups who fought against the Japanese. Many of these partisans in [European] colonies kept their weapons and kept on fighting after the Japanese surrendered. The Vietnamese had to first defeat their former colonial masters, the French, and then take on the United States. The largest of these wars was in China, where the Chinese Communists received the bulk of the Japanese weapons and equipment the Soviets captured when Japanese forces in Manchuria were overrun. China had been embroiled in fighting between Japanese troops and various Chinese factions for most of the 1930s. The fighting didn't end until 1948 when the Chinese Communists triumphed."

of political freedoms, provided voting rights for all adults, and allowed women to own property for the first time in Japan's history. Significantly, most Japanese were pleased by these changes. Article Nine of the new constitution was especially important. It stated that "the Japanese people forever renounce war as a sovereign right of the nation and the threat or use of force as a means of settling international disputes."[92] In effect, the Allies had stripped Japan of its military strength and allowed it to maintain only a small local defense force.

Other far-reaching new measures transformed Japan. The Americans restructured Japanese industry, allowing production only of non-war-related commodities. Also, the entire educational system underwent reform; the new system deemphasized the teaching of traditional, aggressive ideals and stressed Western methods and courses of study. In addition, there were sweeping land reforms. For centuries most of the land had been owned by a few wealthy individuals, and poor peasants had worked it in exchange for some of the food grown. MacArthur decreed that Japan's millions of peasant farmers could now own their own land. This policy bore almost immediate fruit, as by 1950 more than 90 percent of the country's farms had become thriving independent businesses.

In order to aid in economic reconstruction, thousands of U.S. advisers and business experts traveled to Japan. They taught the Japanese how to set up Western-style businesses and trade their goods on the world market. At the same time, billions of U.S. dollars poured into Japan to help support the rebirth of the nation.

By the time the official Pacific War Treaty went into effect in 1952, Japan had become a true ally and trading partner of its former enemies. This remarkable, almost miraculous transformation was made possible in part by the practical, farsighted

MODERN JAPAN ATTACKS THE BUSINESS WORLD

The modern Japanese are as aggressive and industrious as their World War II predecessors. But today it is the business world and not other nations they seek to conquer. During the Allied occupation and miraculous rebuilding of Japan, the Japanese people learned to channel their considerable energies into the production of useful goods for trade on the world market.

By the 1960s Japanese technology, research, and manufacturing methods had caught up with and in some cases surpassed those of most other countries. Well-built Japanese cars flooded the U.S. market in the 1970s and 1980s, outselling many American models. And Japanese-made electronic products such as stereos, TVs, and compact-disc players now dominate the world electronics market.

Japanese businesspeople also learned to wisely invest the huge profits they made from world trade. In the 1980s Japanese firms bought several giant U.S. companies, office buildings, and other real estate. Some Americans have seen this as a threat to the U.S. economy. But others predict that economic competition will be healthy for both countries. "No matter what happens," quipped one American businessman, "it sure beats shooting at each other."

attitudes of Allied leaders. They believed it was more constructive for all nations concerned if the war's winners helped the losers recover, reasoning that punishing the losers would only hinder economic growth on both sides as well as perpetuate hatred and sow the seeds for future unrest. In that same year, Japan's premier, Shigeru Yoshida, thanked the allies for creating "a magnanimous [generous] peace unparalleled in history." He added, "The Japan of today is no longer the Japan of yesterday. We will not fail your expectations of us as a new nation dedicated to peace, democracy, and freedom."[93]

A New World Order Takes Shape

The events of the immense and far-reaching war in the Pacific helped dramatically to alter the balance of power among nations. First, the United States, because of its giant industrial complex and its sole possession of the atomic bomb, became, for all practical purposes, invincible. In fact, the United States entered the postwar era as unquestionably the most powerful nation in history. Significantly, for the first time in memory, a nation with overwhelming strength did not use it to suppress or conquer others. Instead, the United States sought to use its might to maintain peace and help its former enemies.

But the country's reign as the world's only superpower did not last long. The Soviet Union soon showed that it too was a great power to be reckoned with. The

Soviet leadership had been shrewd. All through the war, the Soviets had concentrated on fighting the Germans and had stayed out of the Pacific War. When the United States finally defeated Japan, however, the Soviets became worried, sensing that they would be left out of important postwar agreements in the Pacific. At midnight on August 8, 1945, therefore, just days before the Japanese surrender, the Soviet Union declared war on Japan. This automatically made the Soviets one of the victors in the war; and since the victors shared in shaping the future politics of the region, the Soviets were now assured a voice in that process.

An even more important development happened in the late 1940s, when the Soviets developed their own atomic bomb. That meant that there were now *two* superpowers in the world. What followed was nearly four decades of cold war—large-scale tension and mistrust between the two nations. Each sought to intimidate the other by building more and better nuclear weapons. Ironically, the device that had been conceived to end World War II became, in peacetime, an object of fear that threatened to engulf the world in nuclear destruction.

A Future Without War?

A more positive development of the post–World War II era was the formation of the United Nations (UN) in 1945. Representatives from fifty-one nations met in San Francisco and drew up an initial charter. The main objective of the organization

The United Nations building in New York. In 1945, fifty-one nations formed the United Nations to bring lasting peace to the world.

was to bring lasting peace to the world. The UN charter opens with the historic line: "We the Peoples of the United Nations [are] determined to save succeeding generations from the scourge of war, which twice in our lifetime has brought untold sorrow to mankind."[94]

Other aims of the UN are to uphold fundamental human rights, to maintain international law, and to promote social progress and better living standards. By 1989 membership in the UN had grown to 159 countries. The organization continues to work for the improvement of international relations, striving to fulfill the hope voiced by MacArthur that a better world might emerge out of the blood and carnage of the past.

This was the same hope expressed by Winston Churchill in the darkest days of the great global conflict. The world now had a chance, he said, of avoiding the errors of previous generations. People were crying out for peace, and Allied leaders must recognize the dream of the poor and underprivileged everywhere—to be able to live in peace, protected by governments committed to fighting aggression and evil.

Unfortunately, this hope of MacArthur, Churchill, and others who lived through the agony of World War II remains largely unfulfilled. There have been many other armed conflicts in the world since 1945, including wars in Korea, Vietnam, and the Persian Gulf, as well as the ongoing conflict between the globe's civilized nations and organized terrorists like those who destroyed New York's World Trade Center towers on September 11, 2001. Some people say this proves that war and human strife are inevitable.

Yet others say this idea that there will always be war assumes that humanity will never progress. They have hope that all peoples will someday learn to refrain from using wars like the one fought in the Pacific sphere to solve disputes. Many believe that, given enough time, the civilized nations of the world will become increasingly effective in achieving the momentous goal of preventing war. As Louis Snyder puts it, "For those who believe in human progress there is the hope that, despite the fears and insecurity of the present, there may be a better future."[95]

Notes

Introduction: A Dangerous Clash of National Attitudes

1. Quoted in John Costello, *The Pacific War.* New York: Rawson, Wade, 1981, p. 4.

2. Gordon W. Prange, *At Dawn We Slept: The Untold Story of Pearl Harbor.* New York: McGraw-Hill, 1981, pp. 35–36.

3. Quoted in Prange, *At Dawn We Slept,* p. 36.

Chapter 1: Sons of the Rising Sun: The Long Road to War

4. Edwin O. Reischauer, *The Japanese.* Cambridge, MA: Harvard University Press, 1977, p. 53.

5. Neil F. Busch, *The Horizon Concise History of Japan.* New York: American Heritage, 1972, p. 78.

6. Quoted in Louis L. Snyder, *The War: A Concise History, 1939–1945.* New York: Dell, 1960, p. 50.

7. Quoted in Snyder, *The War,* p. 50.

8. Edwin P. Hoyt, *Japan's War: The Great Pacific Conflict, 1853–1952.* New York: McGraw-Hill, 1986, p. 218.

Chapter 2: "Climb Mount Niitaka": The Attack on Pearl Harbor

9. Quoted in Ronald H. Spector, *Eagle Against the Sun: The American War with Japan.* New York: Free Press, 1985, p. 94.

10. Spector, *Eagle Against the Sun,* p. 95.

11. Quoted in Walter Lord, *Day of Infamy.* 1957. Reprint, New York: Henry Holt, 2001, p. 48.

12. Quoted in Prange, *At Dawn We Slept,* p. 393.

13. Quoted in Prange, *At Dawn We Slept,* p. 379.

14. Quoted in Costello, *Pacific War,* p. 135.

15. Quoted in Prange, *At Dawn We Slept,* p. 507.

16. Quoted in Prange, *At Dawn We Slept,* p. 507.

17. Lord, *Day of Infamy,* pp. 97–98.

18. Quoted in Costello, *Pacific War,* p. 136.

19. Quoted in Costello, *Pacific War,* p. 140.

20. Quoted in Snyder, *The War,* p. 259.

21. Quoted in Snyder, *The War,* p. 258.

22. Quoted in Snyder, *The War,* p. 259.

23. Quoted in Costello, *Pacific War,* p. 141.

24. Quoted in Diane Ravitch, ed., *The American Reader: Words That Moved a Nation.* New York: HarperCollins, 1990, p. 284.

25. Quoted in Snyder, *The War,* p. 263.

26. Quoted in Snyder, *The War,* p. 260.

27. Winston Churchill, *The Second World War.* 6 vols. New York: Bantam, 1962, vol. 3, p. 511.

Chapter 3: From Batavia to Bataan: The Japanese Empire Expands

28. James F. Dunnigan and Albert A. Nofi, *Dirty Little Secrets of World War II.* New York: William Morrow, 1994, p. 285.

29. Quoted in Snyder, *The War,* p. 271.

30. Quoted in Snyder, *The War,* pp. 271–72.

31. Quoted in Spector, *Eagle Against the Sun,* p. 128.

32. Quoted in Snyder, *The War,* p. 275.

33. Quoted in Costello, *Pacific War,* p. 213.

34. Quoted in Costello, *Pacific War,* p. 213.

35. James F. Dunnigan and Albert A. Nofi, *Victory at Sea: World War II in the Pacific.* New York: William Morrow, 1995, p. 16.

36. Spector, *Eagle Against the Sun*, p. 155.

Chapter 4: Turning Point at Midway: The United States Strikes Back

37. Costello, *Pacific War*, p. 246.

38. Quoted in Walter Lord, *Incredible Victory.* New York: Harper and Row, 1967, p. 119.

39. Quoted in Lord, *Incredible Victory*, p. 128.

40. Quoted in Costello, *Pacific War*, p. 296.

41. Quoted in Costello, *Pacific War*, p. 310.

42. Roger V. Daniels, *The Decision to Relocate the Japanese Americans.* Philadelphia: Lippincott, 1975, p. 12.

43. Quoted in Daniel S. Davis, *Behind the Barbed Wire: The Imprisonment of Japanese Americans During World War II.* New York: E.P. Dutton, 1982, p. 30.

44. Congress established the Commission on Wartime Relocation and Internment of Civilians (CWRIC) in 1980 to investigate the World War II detention of Japanese Americans. The CWRIC concluded that the cause had been "race prejudice, war hysteria, and a failure of political leadership" and recommended a payment of $20,000 to each internee. In 1988 the CWRIC's recommendations became law, and in 1990 President George Bush apologized, saying in part, "A monetary sum and words alone cannot restore lost years or erase painful memories. . . . We can never fully right the wrongs of the past. But we can take a clear stand . . . and recognize that serious injustices were done." Quoted from Jerry Stanley, *I Am an American: A True Story of Japanese Internment.* New York: Crown, 1994, p. 90.

45. Snyder, *The War*, p. 294.

46. Quoted in Snyder, *The War*, p. 338.

Chapter 5: "In Death There Is Life": Japan's Desperate Defensive

47. Dunnigan and Nofi, *Dirty Little Secrets*, pp. 283–84.

48. Spector, *Eagle Against the Sun*, pp. 257–58.

49. Harry A. Gailey, *The War in the Pacific.* Novato, CA: Presidio, 1995, p. 312.

50. Quoted in Costello, *Pacific War*, p. 484.

51. Quoted in Snyder, *The War*, p. 558.

52. Quoted in Costello, *Pacific War*, p. 510.

53. Quoted in Snyder, *The War*, p. 560.

54. Quoted in Costello, *Pacific War*, p. 513.

55. Quoted in Snyder, *The War*, p. 560.

56. Quoted in Costello, *Pacific War*, p. 516.

57. Samuel E. Morison, *Oxford History of the American People.* New York: Oxford University Press, 1965, p. 1036.

58. Quoted in Snyder, *The War*, p. 561.

59. Quoted in Snyder, *The War*, p. 568.

60. Quoted in Snyder, *The War*, p. 576.

61. Quoted in Costello, *Pacific War*, p. 546.

62. From a personal interview with the author on October 28, 1990.

63. Quoted in Snyder, *The War*, p. 523.

64. Quoted in Morison, *Oxford History of the American People,* p. 1051.

Chapter 6: Nuclear Dawn: The United States Drops the Atomic Bomb

65. Quoted in William Manchester, *American Caesar: Douglas MacArthur 1880–1964.* London: Arrow Books, 1979, p. 400.

66. Quoted in Roger Bruns, *Almost History: Close Calls, Plan B's, and Twists of Fate in American History.* New York: Hyperion, 2000, pp. 65–66.

67. Quoted in Snyder, *The War*, p. 596.

68. Quoted in John Toland, *The Rising Sun: The Decline and Fall of the Japanese Empire, 1936–1945.* Vol. 2. New York: Random House, 1970, p. 947.

69. Quoted in Toland, *Rising Sun,* p. 949.

70. Quoted in Toland, *Rising Sun,* p. 952.

71. Quoted in Fletcher Knebel and Charles W. Bailey, *No High Ground.* New York: Bantam, 1960, p. 188.

72. Quoted in Spector, *Eagle Against the Sun,* p. 90.

73. Quoted in Costello, *Pacific War,* p. 587, 588.

74. Quoted in Costello, *Pacific War,* p. 591.

75. Quoted in Knebel and Bailey, *No High Ground,* pp. 158–59.

76. Quoted in Costello, *Pacific War,* p. 591.

77. Quoted in Hans Dollinger, *The Decline and Fall of Nazi Germany and Imperial Japan.* New York: Bonanza Books, 1967, p. 387.

78. Toland, *Rising Sun,* p. 973.

79. Quoted in Snyder, *The War,* pp. 602–3.

80. Quoted in Snyder, *The War,* pp. 602–3.

81. Quoted in Knebel and Bailey, *No High Ground,* pp. 178–79.

82. Quoted in Dollinger, *Decline and Fall,* p. 388.

Chapter 7: "That Peace Be Now Restored": Surrender and Aftermath

83. Quoted in Toland, *Rising Sun,* p. 999.

84. Quoted in Toland, *Rising Sun,* pp. 1005–6.

85. Quoted in Spector, *Eagle Against the Sun,* p. 556.

86. Quoted in Toland, *Rising Sun,* p. 1011.

87. Quoted in Toland, *Rising Sun,* pp. 1028–29.

88. Quoted in Hoyt, *Japan's War,* p. 438.

89. Quoted in Costello, *Pacific War,* p. 600.

90. Quoted in Costello, *Pacific War,* p. 601.

91. Quoted in Snyder, *The War,* p. 606.

92. Quoted in Hoyt, *Japan's War,* p. 452.

93. Quoted in Snyder, *The War,* p. 645.

94. See the *Encyclopedia Britannica* or any other major encyclopedia under "United Nations."

95. Snyder, *The War,* p. 654.

For Further Reading

Mary Virginia Fox, *The Importance of Douglas MacArthur*. San Diego: Lucent Books, 1999. Well organized and well researched, this is perhaps the best biography for young adults of the famous and controversial American general who had to abandon the Philippines to the Japanese but later returned and drove them out.

Ann Graham Gaines, *Commodore Perry Opens Japan to Trade in World History*. Berkeley Heights, NJ: Enslow, 2000. An excellent study for young people of Perry's nineteenth-century expedition to Japan designed to force the Japanese into the world community. This material is essential for understanding the Japanese character and why Japan resented the Western nations.

R.G. Grant, *Hiroshima and Nagasaki*. New York: Raintree Steck/Vaughn, 1998. Describes the events leading up to the dropping of two atomic bombs on Japan in 1945, as well as the devastation they created and the way they changed the world.

Don Nardo, *Franklin D. Roosevelt: U.S. President*. New York: Chelsea House, 1996. A brief but informative synopsis of Roosevelt's life, including his stewardship of the United States during the turbulent years of World War II.

——, *Modern Japan*. San Diego: Lucent Books, 1995. The second half of a two-volume history of Japan, this one begins with the emergence of modern Japan in the 1800s and traces major events and figures through Japan's wars with Russia, China, and the United States.

Patricia D. Netzley, *Japan*. San Diego: Lucent Books, 2000. Part of Lucent's excellent Modern Nations of the World series, this volume provides a considerable amount of general information about Japanese history, culture, society, and people.

Conrad Stein, *The USS Arizona*. New York: Children's Press, 1992. This nicely mounted study of the most famous warship sunk by the Japanese at Pearl Harbor is aimed at junior high and high school readers.

Theodore Taylor, *Air Raid—Pearl Harbor!: The Story of December 7, 1941*. New York: Harcourt Brace, 1991. A very well-written overview of the attack on Pearl Harbor, aimed at junior high school readers.

Diane Yancey, *Life in a Japanese American Internment Camp*. San Diego: Lucent Books, 1998. A very thorough and well-written summary of the shameful episode in which the U.S. government imprisoned some of its own citizens because of an irrational fear that they might collaborate with the enemy. Highly recommended.

Works Consulted

John Costello, *The Pacific War.* New York: Rawson, Wade, 1981. This large overview of the conflict between the United States and Japan is well written and well informed and contains numerous very useful maps.

Daniel S. Davis, *Behind the Barbed Wire: The Imprisonment of Japanese Americans During World War II.* New York: E.P. Dutton, 1982. An informative and moving examination of one of the country's darkest hours and worst mistakes; namely, its imprisonment of its own citizens based on groundless hysteria.

James F. Dunnigan and Albert A. Nofi, *Victory at Sea: World War II in the Pacific.* New York: William Morrow, 1995. A large, very informative recent overview of the events, logistics, and personalities of the Pacific War.

Joseph C. Grew, *Ten Years in Japan.* New York: Simon & Schuster, 1944. An informative and fascinating account of Japan in the 1930s, especially in politics, as seen through the collected diaries and private and official papers of the author, who served as the U.S. ambassador to Japan from 1932–42.

Edwin P. Hoyt, *Japan's War: The Great Pacific Conflict, 1853–1952.* New York: McGraw-Hill, 1986. Hoyt carefully traces Japanese expansionism, beginning with the Meiji Restoration, and chronicles the collapse of Japan's empire in World War II. He also discusses the American occupation from 1945 to 1952.

Fletcher Knebel and Charles W. Bailey, *No High Ground.* New York: Bantam, 1960. A well-written, detailed journalistic approach to the story of the development and use of the first atomic bombs by the United States.

Walter Lord, *Day of Infamy.* 1957. Reprint, New York: Henry Holt, 2001. One of the best accounts of the Japanese attack on Pearl Harbor.

———, *Incredible Victory.* New York: Harper and Row, 1967. Lord's fine, detailed overview of the Battle of Midway, in which the United States defeated the Japanese and began pushing them westward across the Pacific.

Roger Manvell, *Films and the Second World War.* New York: Dell, 1974. A very informative and readable synopsis of American, British, German, Japanese, and other films made for both propaganda and entertainment purposes during the war.

Gordon W. Prange, *At Dawn We Slept: The Untold Story of Pearl Harbor.* New York: McGraw-Hill, 1981. A massive, well-documented telling of the Pearl Harbor disaster, with hundreds of eyewitness accounts.

Edwin O. Reischauer, *Japan: Past and Present.* New York: Knopf, 1964. A respected scholar said of this book by one of the twentieth century's leading experts on Japan, "I do not know of any short book on Japanese history which gives so much useful information in so brief and simple a form."

————, *The Japanese.* Cambridge, MA: Harvard University Press, 1977. This superb study of Japan uses the country's history to explain how modern Japanese act and think. In his preface Reischauer comments, "I have . . . sought to achieve a wide focus on contemporary Japan as seen in the light of its whole past experience." He succeeds admirably.

Martin J. Sherwin, *A World Destroyed: The Atomic Bomb and the Grand Alliance.* New York: Vintage Books, 1977. A first-rate synopsis of the development of the atomic bomb, its use on Japanese cities, and its political repercussions.

Mamoru Shigemitsu, *Japan and Her Destiny.* New York: Dutton, 1958. A moving account of Japan's military rise and fall told by a fine Japanese historian.

Louis L. Snyder, *The War: A Concise History, 1939–1945.* New York: Dell, 1960. A fast-paced, well-informed brief overview of World War II that also contains a huge collection of excerpts from primary documents collected from numerous American and Japanese sources, a number of which I have quoted.

Ronald H. Spector, *Eagle Against the Sun: The American War with Japan.* New York: Free Press, 1985. Perhaps the finest single-volume account of the entire panorama of the Pacific War available. Spector combines solid scholarship with brilliant analysis and moving prose. Highly recommended.

John Toland, *Infamy: Pearl Harbor and Its Aftermath.* Garden City, NY: Doubleday, 1982. A fast-paced overview of the Pacific War written by one of the twentieth century's leading scholars in the field.

————, *The Rising Sun: The Decline and Fall of the Japanese Empire, 1936–1945.* 2 vols. New York: Random House, 1970. A massive and magnificent telling of the war in the Pacific, filled with detail and meticulously documented. Highly recommended.

Additional Works Consulted

Teruhiko Asada, *The Night of a Thousand Suicides*. New York: St. Martin's Press, 1970.

William T. de Bary, *Sources of Japanese Tradition*. New York: Columbia University Press, 1964.

W.G. Beasley, *The Modern History of Japan*. London: Weidenfeld and Nicolson, 1973.

T.A. Bisson, *Japan's War Economy*. New York: Macmillan, 1945.

Bruce Blevin Jr., *From Pearl Harbor to Okinawa: The War in the Pacific, 1941–1945*. New York: Random House, 1960.

Lester Brooks, *Behind Japan's Surrender*. New York: McGraw-Hill, 1968.

Roger Bruns, *Almost History: Close Calls, Plan B's, and Twists of Fate in American History*. New York: Hyperion, 2000.

Neil F. Busch, *The Horizon Concise History of Japan*. New York: American Heritage, 1972.

Winston Churchill, *The Second World War*. 6 vols. New York: Bantam, 1962.

Roger V. Daniels, *The Decision to Relocate the Japanese Americans*. Philadelphia: Lippincott, 1975.

Ronald E. Dolan and Robert L. Worden, *Japan: A Country Study*. Washington, DC: U.S. Government Printing Office, 1992.

Hans Dollinger, *The Decline and Fall of Nazi Germany and Imperial Japan*. New York: Bonanza Books, 1967.

James F. Dunnigan and Albert A. Nofi, *Dirty Little Secrets of World War II*. New York: William Morrow, 1994.

———, *The Pacific War Encyclopedia*. New York: Facts On File, 1998.

Herbert Feis, *The Road to Pearl Harbor*. Princeton: Princeton University Press, 1950.

Mitsuo Fuchida and Masatake Okumiya, *Midway, the Battle That Doomed Japan*. Annapolis: Naval Institute Press, 1955.

Harry A. Gailey, *The War in the Pacific*. Novato, CA: Presidio, 1995.

Edwin P. Hoyt, *Pacific Destiny*. New York: Norton, 1981.

Robert Lawson, *C/O Fleet P.O.: True Experiences of Marines in the Pacific*. Wilton, CT: Stratotech Graphics, 1998.

Robert Leckie, *Great American Battles*. New York: Random House, 1968.

Ronald Lewin, *The American Magic: Codes, Ciphers, and the Defeat of Japan*. New York: Farrar, Straus, & Giroux, 1982.

Jon Livingston et al. Eds., *The Japan Reader: Postwar Japan, 1945 to the Present*. New York: Random House, 1973.

William Manchester, *American Caesar: Douglas MacArthur, 1880–1964*. London: Arrow Books, 1979.

Milton W. Meyer, *Japan: A Concise History.* Lanham, MD: Rowman & Littlefield, 1993.

Samuel E. Morison, *History of United States Naval Operations in World War II.* 15 vols. Boston: Little, Brown, 1947–62.

———, *Oxford History of the American People.* New York: Oxford University Press, 1965.

W. Scott Morton, *Japan: Its History and Culture.* New York: McGraw-Hill, 1984.

Richard F. Newcomb, *Iwo Jima.* New York: Holt, Rinehart and Winston, 1965.

Diane Ravitch, ed., *The American Reader: Words That Moved a Nation.* New York: HarperCollins, 1990.

Edwin O. Reischauer, *Japan: The Story of a Nation.* New York: Knopf, 1970.

———, *The Japanese Today: Continuity and Change.* Cambridge: Harvard University Press, 1988.

Howard B. Schonberger, *Aftermath of War: Americans and the Remaking of Japan, 1945–1952.* Kent, OH: Kent State University Press, 1989.

Jerry Stanley, *I Am an American: A True Story of Japanese Internment.* New York: Crown, 1994.

Russell C. Stroup, *Letters from the Pacific: A Combat Chaplain in World War II.* Columbia: University of Missouri Press, 2000.

Hakwon Sunoo, *Japanese Militarism, Past and Present.* Chicago: Nelson Hall, 1975.

Index

see also Pearl Harbor;
   West, the
U.S. Pacific Fleet, 29

Valkenburgh, Franklin
   Van, 37

Wainwright, Jonathan M., 51
Wake Island, 40, 45
Waku, Yukio, 46–47
warships. See ships
weapons
   limits placed on
      Japanese, 22–23
   samurai, 18

see also aircraft; ships
West, the
   attitude toward war, 11, 14
   establishing trade
      relations with Japan,
      20–21
   Japanese opinion on,
      12–13
   limiting Japanese power,
      22–23
   response to Japanese acts
      of aggression, 23, 26
   see also Great Britain;
      United States
West Virginia (warship), 29

women, labor by, 70–71
World War I, 26
World War II, 11
   see also Pacific War

Yamamoto, Isoroku, 56
   Midway campaign and,
      57–58, 59, 66
   raid on Tokyo and, 57
Yamato (warship), 85
Yoritomo, Minamoto,
   16–17
Yugoslavia, 43

Zero (fighter plane), 31

Picture Credits

Cover Photo: Digital Stock

© Paul Almasy/CORBIS, 112

© Bettmann/CORBIS, 13, 34, 84, 90, 100 (both), 101, 103, 106

© CORBIS, 10 (right), 25, 40, 41, 47, 53, 56, 67, 72, 76 (left), 81, 83, 93, 94

Digital Stock, 39, 51, 57, 71, 76 (right), 80, 86, 98, 107

© Hulton Archive, 10 (left), 12

© Hulton-Deutsch Collection/CORBIS, 24, 54

Chris Jouan, 63, 65, 77

Library of Congress, 11, 37, 43 (left), 64, 97

© The Mariner's Museum/CORBIS, 43 (right)

© Museum of Flight/CORBIS, 31

National Japanese American Historical Society, 69, 70

North Wind Picture Archives, 17, 19

Martha Schierholz, 30, 33, 36, 50, 92

About the Author

Historian and award-winning author Don Nardo has written many books for young adults about American history and government, including *The U.S. Presidency, The Declaration of Independence, The Bill of Rights, The Great Depression, Franklin D. Roosevelt: U.S. President,* and *The Mexican-American War.* He has also published a two-volume history of Japan for young adults. Mr. Nardo lives with his wife, Christine, in Massachusetts.